VIRTUAL REFERENCE BEST PRACTICES

TAILORING SERVICES TO YOUR LIBRARY

M. KATHLEEN KERN

AMERICAN LIBRARY ASSOCIATION

CHICAGO   2009

M. Kathleen Kern, MSLIS, is the digital services coordinator in central reference services at the University of Illinois at Urbana. She co-manages the library's virtual reference service, which has offered chat since 2001 and instant messaging since 2005. She is a past chair of RUSA's Machine Assisted Reference Section (MARS) within ALA and co-chaired the committee that authored the Guidelines for Implementing and Maintaining Virtual Reference Services. Her interests are assessment of library services and integration of virtual reference with more traditional reference services.

Library of Congress Cataloging-in-Publication Data
Kern, M. Kathleen.
Virtual reference best practices : tailoring services to your library / M. Kathleen Kern.
p.   cm.
Includes bibliographical references and index.
ISBN 978-0-8389-0975-1 (alk. paper)
1. Electronic reference services (Libraries) I. Title.
Z711.45K47 2009
025.5'2—dc22   2008015379

ISBN-13: 978-0-8389-0975-1

Printed in the United States of America

13 12 11 10 09   5 4 3 2 1

contents

acknowledgments

I wish to acknowledge the Research and Publication Committee of the University of Illinois at Urbana-Champaign Library, which provided support for the completion of this research. I truly could not have done this without the support provided, particularly the funding to hire Lena Singer (BA in journalism and MSLIS, both from the University of Illinois), who conducted many interviews, wrote research summaries, and tracked down supporting facts.

Many people consented to write Library Field Reports. They are credited with their reports, but I would like to thank them individually here, for I know the time writing a thousand words can demand: Michael Gorman and Mark McCullough, Michelle Maloney, Alec Sonsteby, Melissa Records, and Wayne Bivens-Tatum.

Many more librarians took the time to be interviewed. In the end, some interviews resulted in full-length field reports and others were used only in part. Reading the interviews was one of the best parts of writing this book. The variety in implementations of virtual reference is why I started it, and the range of experiences shared with me by other librarians is what propelled me to keep writing.

Thanks to my editor Kelli Christiansen at bibliobibuli not only for having a great company name but for asking me the right questions and providing the necessary prodding toward the goal.

Most important, I cannot express enough thanks to my husband Shea for providing chocolate, putting up with my late-night writing habits, and giving up spending time with me. His support and confidence in me made writing this book possible.

introduction

*I*n 2004, the Reference and User Services Association of the American Library Association introduced the Guidelines for Implementing and Maintaining Virtual Reference Services (VR Guidelines) in response to the growth of virtual reference services and increased demand from libraries for direction in setting up and operating this new type of patron service.

The VR Guidelines meet this need by providing a checklist of decision points regarding the implementation. Many librarians have been surprised that these guidelines do not prescribe particular models for establishing a virtual reference service. The committee that drafted the guidelines intentionally left room for variation in local practice. Just as there is great variety in the ways libraries of different size, type, organizational structure, and user population offer in-person reference, so it was expected that variety would exist in virtual reference and that over time, as this new service matured, multiple best practices would emerge. The committee's philosophy was confirmed during the VR Guidelines open comment period. Librarians spoke out vocally about best practices that they felt should be included in the VR Guidelines, but these practices often were in direct opposition to one another. What worked for one library would prohibit the support of a service for another. It was decided that the guidelines would be informative but not overly prescriptive. As a result, the VR Guidelines are a useful framework for decision making, but they leave space for virtual reference implementation to fit the needs of each library and user community.

This book bridges the space between the VR Guidelines and implementation at your library by providing a process for making the decisions recommended in the guidelines. For example, where the VR Guidelines indicate that a library policy "should be established for determining which queries fall outside the parameters of service, and how to respond in those cases," this book contains exercises your library may use to determine a virtual reference service policy.

Key to a successful implementation is that you design your virtual reference service to fit the particular needs of your patrons and your library organization. To that end, although this book is not a collection of research findings, it does include examples from other libraries and occasionally research reports that should be practical and informative to your local decision making.

Integration of virtual reference with traditional reference services is an underlying theme of the VR Guidelines. Integration means planning for virtual reference as a long-term service, not as an add-on. It is mainstreaming virtual reference into a library's operations, budget, and assessments.

Sustainability of virtual reference services has become an issue: some services have started, only to fold within a couple of years or a few months. Good planning combined with an integrated approach to virtual reference will not guarantee a strong and enduring service, but they are critical components to success.

Using This Book

This book is meant to move you and your library from the abstract, checklist format of the VR Guidelines to the concrete decision making that you need in order to start and manage virtual reference service at your library. Information in this book is presented in five basic ways:

Narrative text explains the decisions a library needs to make to start a virtual reference service, the process and components necessary to make decisions that fit your library, and some background on what other libraries are doing.

Exercises provide a concrete framework for the decision-making process. Most major library decisions are made by committees, teams, or working groups. These exercises are keys to focusing on one decision at a time, in a logical progression, and bringing the group together while allowing individuals a voice in the process. The exercises are formatted for easy photocopying. If you are a solo decision maker, the exercises will still be useful in provoking and organizing your thoughts.

Worksheets often are used in conjunction with exercises and are a place to collect data for decision making. They also are formatted for photocopying.

Library Field Reports highlight practices of virtual reference at specific libraries; they are included as fodder for discussion and thought. Remember: what is a best practice at one library may not fit your library organization or clientele, but these examples should lead to consideration of the issues at hand.

Research You Can Use sections are one-page synopses of significant research in the area of virtual reference with an emphasis on how the research is of practical importance to libraries. These are included for reflection and guidance and are formatted to be easily copied.

The structure of the book is loosely based on the VR Guidelines, and I encourage you to refer to the guidelines as your library works through the decision-making process outlined in this book. The VR Guidelines are provided in appendix A. Appendix C is a checklist of decisions intended to help ensure that all components vital to the successful implementation of a virtual reference service are in place.

There are several ways that your library can structure the decision-making process. Your library may wish to have weekly meetings and tackle one decision at each meeting. Or, it may be more your style to bring people together for half-days to make several decisions. Exercises might be done in preparation for a meeting or as part of the in-person discussion. I make recommendations throughout where I have a preference, but flexibility to fit your library is the key to success even in planning. If I recommend a three-hour workshop but that is out of the question for your staff, then more frequent shorter meetings will have to be the answer. Make the decisions that fit *your* library.

CHAPTER 1

Defining Virtual Reference

You probably have read and heard several different terms that are related to virtual reference—or that you think may be related to virtual reference. I cannot set standard nomenclature, but there are some terms I prefer and use consistently throughout this book. Most of my preferences are based on a long history with this area of reference, working on the VR Guidelines, and involvement with the Virtual Reference Desk Conference.

Terms in This Book

Virtual Reference

This is the first definition listed because virtual reference is the central concept of this book (see figure 1-1). The definition below is from the VR Guidelines. It is a good definition that is as accurate today as it was when it was written in 2004:

> Virtual reference is reference service initiated electronically, often in real-time, where patrons employ computers or other Internet technology to communicate with reference staff, without being physically present. Communication channels used frequently in virtual reference include chat, videoconferencing, Voice over IP, co-browsing, e-mail, and instant messaging.

In practice, sometimes librarians say "virtual reference" when they are talking specifically about chat, or IM, or e-mail. Virtual reference is a concept apart from the technology that supports it, so when someone says "virtual reference" they could be referring to any number of technologies. I've read articles supposedly about virtual reference that turned out—halfway through the article—to be about e-mail only. To avoid such confusion in these pages, I am specific when it is needed: if a section is only about e-mail or only about chat, then that is the term I use. If a decision point is relevant only to e-mail, I specify e-mail. When I use the term *virtual reference*, it is because the concept being explored pertains to any virtual service.

FIGURE 1-1 TOOLS FOR VIRTUAL REFERENCE

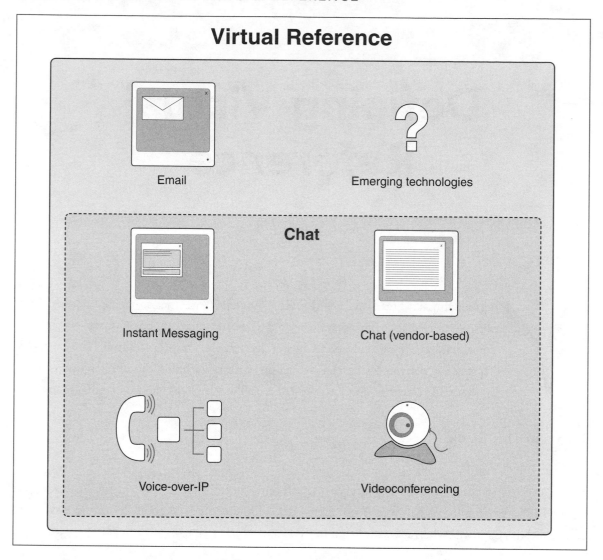

Chat

Chat can be accomplished by using different types of software, but the distinguishing characteristics are the "live" (real-time or synchronous) nature of the communication and that it is electronically facilitated, generally using typed text transmitted computer to computer.

If you were reading this sentence on your computer screen while I was keyboarding it on my laptop, that would be chatting. Chat is a two-way communication, so you would be able to type a message back to me that I would be reading right now.

When I use the term *chat*, I am referring to synchronous virtual communication, commercial chat software, or instant messaging.

Instant Messaging

Instant messaging is quite similar to chat in that it is text-based and computer-facilitated. The difference is in the software used. These differences are explored in more detail in chapter 6.

If I am writing specifically about instant messaging, and not about other chat software, then I use the terms *IM* or *instant messaging.*

Collaborative Virtual Reference

Collaborative virtual reference is a joint venture between two or more libraries to offer a single or shared virtual reference service to their patrons. There are many types of consortial arrangements, which I review in chapter 10. You may also see this referred to as *cooperative virtual reference* elsewhere, but I stick to one term.

E-mail

E-mail is the most common and oldest of the virtual reference communication tools. Libraries have been using e-mail for reference service for more than twenty years. E-mail allows users to send a message any time to a person who may or may not be online at the same time. The message will be read some time after it has been sent, so in this sense back-and-forth e-mail communication is similar to letters written on paper (but without as long a delivery delay). E-mail is, therefore, an asynchronous service.

Synchronous Virtual Reference

Synchronous virtual reference can refer to chat, IM, videoconferencing—any computer-mediated communication that occurs in real time. Although accurate, it is a cumbersome term. Usually, when I am writing about synchronous virtual services I use *chat* as the generic term.

Asynchronous Virtual Reference

Asynchronous virtual reference refers to computer-mediated communication that is sent by one person and received at a different time by the recipient. This includes e-mail and text messaging. In this book, I most frequently use the more specific terms *e-mail* or *text messaging.*

VR Guidelines

There are many guidelines, but the guidelines for this book are the Guidelines for Implementing and Maintaining Virtual Reference Services, the VR Guidelines. These were published by the Reference and User Services Association of the American Library Association in 2004.

Other guidelines may be of interest, such as those from IFLA, the International Federation of Library Associations. Some are listed at the end of appendix A.

Text Messaging

Text messaging is communication via text to or from a mobile phone. The text may be received by a user with another mobile phone, or it can be sent to e-mail or even an IM account. This interoperability allows users with different preferences and electronic devices to send and receive text. It is typically limited to 160 characters (see SMS, below).

SMS

SMS, or Short Message Service, is text transmitted to or from a digital mobile phone. See *Text Messaging*, above. The SMS protocol limits the length of an individual message to 160 characters, including spaces.

To give you a sense of how many characters there are in a typical paragraph, the above definition is 212 characters.

Vendor-Based Chat

Vendor-based chat is a term used to distinguish between virtual reference that uses chat software (which is most often purchased from a vendor) and that which uses software and services based on use of IM. There is more detail on this topic in chapter 6.

Videoconferencing or Videochat

Videochat includes transmission of a live video of each person (provided both have the necessary camera hardware) along with the typed text. It can be combined with VoIP (Voice-over-Internet Protocol) so that both picture and sound are sent via computer. Videoconferencing is the more traditional telephone plus video, which requires rather unique equipment on both ends of the communication. A few libraries have forayed into this area of service.

Terms Not Used in This Book

Digital Reference

Digital reference is another term used for the concept of *virtual reference*, and they are often used synonymously. *Digital reference* seems to have been more popular several years ago, with *virtual reference* the more common term now. I do not use *digital reference* because it is open to confusion with the digital resources that libraries use. So, you won't see the term *digital reference* in this book, but you will encounter it in other things written about virtual reference.

Electronic Reference

This term is even more ambiguous than *digital reference*. The most common use of *electronic reference* is when talking about online resources such as electronic encyclopedias. Be aware that some writers may use this as a synonym for *virtual reference;* you will need to ascertain meaning from context.

CHAPTER 2

Implementing Virtual Reference

IS IT THE RIGHT THING, RIGHT NOW?

The most important decision about starting a virtual reference service is the decision to start. Or to not start. This may seem surprising to read in a book about implementing virtual reference, but it is possible that you will decide that virtual reference is not right for your library, or that it's not right for your library right now. This book is about making decisions that fit *your library*. Part of planning a successful service is making informed, sound decisions at the outset, starting with the very basics of why this service and why right now.

Undoubtedly you have heard or read quite a bit about virtual reference. The buzz about it does not seem to be fading. New technologies and the "Net Generation" have kept this issue at the forefront of library services. In this chapter, I provide reasons why virtual reference seems like the right thing, right now for a lot of libraries. But the focus of this book is on your library. Only your library can decide (and needs to decide) if virtual reference is where you want to focus your energy at this time. So, I also provide some reasons why a library might decide to not implement virtual reference, or to defer the decision. Most important, there is an exercise to guide your library in its discussion about virtual reference.

A Few Good Reasons

Reach Out and IM Someone: Communication and the Net Generation

Electronic communication is amazingly popular with the age cohort referred to as the Millennial Generation—those born between the years 1982 and 2000.[1] This group is also sometimes referred to as the Net Generation for their propensity toward electronic communication, use of the Internet, and online gaming. They prefer IM over the telephone—and this includes the cell phone. Most teenagers report talking to multiple people via IM at the same time—that is individual, simultaneous IM conversations, not group conversations.[2] Keep that in mind for later when considering chat communication.

E-mail remains a vital tool for communication in business and personal life and is used by more than 89 percent of all people who are online, across all age groups, in the United States. E-mail is a viable virtual reference option, especially when the target age group is older or may prefer to "drop off" their question and receive a response later. This may be the case with libraries attempting to provide research or market literature search results, as is often the case with special libraries. However, e-mail is seen by many Millennials as too slow. Among those 12–17-year-olds, 75 percent of those who go online use IM. They still use e-mail, but they prefer IM to communicate with friends.[3] By contrast, of online young adults ages 18–28, 66 percent use IM. These numbers continue to drop in the older age groups.[4]

Interestingly, the Pew reports reported above do not ask about vendor-based chat communications—basically because this type of chat has not been adopted by the general population. It is a tool of e-commerce and libraries. Retailers as varied as the outdoor company Backcountry (www.backcountry.com) and Vosges Haute Chocolate (www.vosgeschocolate.com) employ it with great success for assisting customers with online orders. More than two thousand libraries are part of the QuestionPoint consortium, and an untold number reach their users through other chat services such as Tutor.com, Docutek VRplus, or shareware chat programs.

We need not examine the different attributes and uses of each software type now. What is important as a starting point for consideration of a virtual reference service is that library users (and nonusers) are researching and communicating online.

New Audiences: Not Just Millennials Anymore

As demonstrated by the Pew data cited above, it is not just the under-25 group that is reached by virtual reference. E-mail already is a popular communication tool and one in use at many libraries. As IM gains acceptance as a mode of communication in some parts of people's lives, it is likely that they will adopt it for other uses. The telephone started out with what today would be considered low market saturation. It was uncommon for people to use it in their private lives for anything other than emergencies or brief communication with distant relatives. It was a tool for conducting business. The telephone took decades to become a fixture at most library reference desks; it took private phone lines being common in the American household first.[5]

The Vancouver Public Library found that when it started offering chat reference in 2003 it was reaching patrons who had never asked a question at a reference desk in person or via telephone. A survey revealed that 16–21 percent of the users of the library's chat reference service had never asked a question of that library via telephone, e-mail, or in person.[6] For a library to reach a nonuser population is a major success and evidence of tapping an unmet need, whatever the age group of the patron.

Seizing an Opportunity

Some libraries have started chat reference service because the timing seemed right. Perhaps an opportunity opened to join a consortium; software may have been offered at a discounted price, providing an incentive to try chat as a pilot; the state library may have been providing all training and marketing during the first year; and so forth. Events that lower the barriers to implementing a new virtual reference service can be the opportunity your library has been waiting for. These offers often come from the state library or from a library consortium in which your library already participates. It never hurts to inquire with your consortium or to approach a network of which your library is not yet a member.

Generate Some Buzz

Probably not a good reason on its own, creating something to talk about is a good secondary reason for starting virtual reference. For example, the opening of a new library building typically increases visits to the library and positively affects circulation. Similarly, a well-marketed virtual reference service can create some goodwill toward the library and increase reference inquiries. It can increase the perception of the library as a vibrant and forward-looking place, one in touch with its community.

Not So Good, but Not Uncommon, Reasons

Bandwagonism

This is the "everyone else is doing it" mentality. Fear of not keeping up, of being the last one to adopt, is the motivation behind this reason for starting a virtual reference service or adopting a new technology. Some libraries are even early adopters of a new technology so that they are among the first to be on a growing trend. This is an insufficient reason for starting any project. It does not guarantee success. Success comes by seeing if there are other, more solid, reasons for your library to implement virtual reference.

Peer Pressure

Libraries have peers, and sometimes they exert pressure or influence. A library wishing to start or expand a virtual reference consortium may try to persuade other libraries of the necessity of being part of the movement. A regional agency may try to gain complete participation from all of its member libraries. As mentioned above, seizing the opportunities and incentives that these groups provide to start a new service can be an advantage to your library. On the other hand, avoid having a decision made for you. It is still important that the service be a good fit for your library and that it be implemented in a way that makes sense to your organization and your patrons.

Something to Do

Doing something just for the sake of having something new to do may look good on a personal or library annual report, but it is unlikely to lead to a lasting and successful service. Professional boredom and library stagnation can be alleviated with many activities. Be sure that virtual reference is the best answer for a new project and more than just something to do.

Every Issue Has Two Sides

Of course, there are also disadvantages to implementing virtual reference, which we examine more thoroughly throughout the book. For example, we consider appropriateness to your library's

TABLE 2-1 PROS AND CONS OF IMPLEMENTING VIRTUAL REFERENCE

Possible advantages	Possible disadvantages
Reach online users	Additional costs of operation (staff, software, etc.)
Reach previous nonusers	Staff resistance
Point-of-need assistance	Other, more urgent, priorities
Take advantage of software trial period (if offered by a consortium)	Not appropriate for your community
Publicity for all services	

audience in chapter 3. Table 2-1 lists some of the pros and cons associated with implementing virtual reference. You may be able to think of others. Some of these factors are more important than others, and this too varies from library to library. Some of the issues may not apply to your library. Some of the seeming disadvantages may be overcome with creativity.

Library Readiness

The considerations mentioned above approach virtual reference from the service standpoint because it is the mission of a library to be a service for its community: who are your patrons, and is virtual reference a service they are likely to use? But it is also necessary to look at the readiness of the library as an organization before committing to a new endeavor—keeping in mind, of course, that patron considerations are where we start because that is what should be most compelling in our decision making.

Is This Our Priority?

There are always services and projects competing for your library's limited resources. Everything a library wants to do, even those things it considers important priorities, cannot be accomplished at once.

How many projects can your library do at once? This depends on the size and duration of the project, and on which staff are involved. Simultaneous projects and a virtual reference service will not conflict if they do not draw too heavily on the same staff. A new adult literacy initiative and summer reading program will not conflict too much in a library with separate children's and adult services staff. But virtual reference implementation and either of the mentioned programs might draw on the same staff. If you expect your virtual reference service to be targeted as a homework help service, planning for your children's staff to lend a lot of time during the spring when they are preparing for summer reading is unwise.

Money is a perpetual consideration. Even with implementations that have a negligible software cost, there will be costs for marketing and perhaps for training and hardware. Staff time also costs money. In addition to pulling current staff away from other responsibilities, a new virtual reference service many require additional staffing; the precise impact on staffing depends on your model for operating the service.

Too much going on at once is an abstract, but real, issue. Aside from money and staff, there is only so much your library can promote at the same time. So, even if multiple projects are in the planning, rollouts and marketing should be staggered. Give each project space to be in the spotlight.

Worksheet 2-1 asks you to list other projects that are in process at your library as well as those things that are priorities but perhaps not yet in the planning stages. Unless yours is a small library, you will either need to confer with your co-workers (across departments) or ask several people to complete the worksheet.

This worksheet is just a data collection form. The data will help you (or the implementation group) decide if now is the right time to implement a virtual reference service. Collecting a list of who is involved in other projects reveals availability for this implementation. Sometimes people are willing to commit but unable to contribute the needed time. Knowing their other obligations ahead of time can help with knowing who to ask, as well as helping those who can't say "no" to assess their time accurately.

Remember that not all projects are visible to patrons or even to other library staff. Some are internal to a department, such as a staff reconfiguration or a new workflow for a core process. Other projects are library-wide but not aimed at patrons, like strategic planning activities. These projects are as important to collect as the more obvious public-focused projects.

In worksheet 2-1, priorities are those things that are future projects. They may be under investigation right now or awaiting time, money, or a new hire. These priorities do not yet have a time line, but it is necessary to know about them in order to fit virtual reference implementation into the project queue.

Timing is different from need. If there is too much going on right now, but virtual reference is a priority, use the data to determine a more feasible time line to start the service.

What about Me?

Much of this book is about the library and its decisions related to internal issues such as staffing, assessment, and training. Pay attention to proposals for which staff needs and user needs may conflict. Be open to compromise: user needs may come first in some decisions, and staff needs may prove most important in others. Smooth implementation necessitates staff knowing that this is a service designed around changing user behavior, but also that the needs of staff are an important part of the process.

As an example of an activity for which staff and patron needs may be at odds, consider this scenario regarding hours of operation. Your users have expressed an interest in longer hours of operation, and virtual reference may seem a way to achieve this. Although it will cost less to have librarians answer virtual reference questions from home than keeping the entire library open, there are several staff and patron issues to consider:

> ➤ Librarian work days may need to be longer; if total work hours are to remain the same, where will staff working hours be reduced?

> ➤ Is there enthusiasm from staff about working reference from home? Some may appreciate the opportunity to work a late evening and have a morning off. Are enough people interested in this work arrangement? If not, are there other ways to offer extended hours of service?

WORKSHEET 2-1 OTHER PROJECTS AND PRIORITIES

Library _____ Date _____

PROJECT DESCRIPTION	NEW OPAC INTERFACE
Audience	All patrons
Primary staff involved	Library IT manager, OPAC team (asst. head of reference, serials cataloger, circulation supervisor, volunteer shelver)
Other staff affected	All public services staff (heavily), all cataloging staff (minimally)
Implementation time line	New OPAC in place July 2008 (three months from now). Training for staff in late June 2008.
Possible conflicts with virtual reference / considerations for time line	May–July for OPAC team members VR training: not June July rollout for OPAC makes July bad for VR rollout (for staff)? June or July VR service might be good for patrons with OPAC questions?

PROJECT DESCRIPTION	
Audience	
Primary staff involved	
Other staff affected	
Implementation time line	
Possible conflicts with virtual reference / considerations for time line	

PROJECT DESCRIPTION	
Audience	
Primary staff involved	
Other staff affected	
Implementation time line	
Possible conflicts with virtual reference / considerations for time line	

PROJECT DESCRIPTION	
Audience	
Primary staff involved	
Other staff affected	
Implementation time line	
Possible conflicts with virtual reference / considerations for time line	

Etc. as needed

FUTURE PRIORITY	FEDERATED SEARCHING
Audience	YA-adult patrons
Primary staff involved	Head of cataloging and implementation team with two reference librarians and head of IT
Immediacy	High importance, long time line
Awaiting resources?	Arrival of new head of cataloging
Possible conflicts with virtual reference / considerations for time line	High planning commitment from reference staff Training may be intense No product has been identified; this committee is not likely to form for another two months with a completion date in over a year

FUTURE PRIORITY	
Audience	
Primary staff involved	
Immediacy	
Awaiting resources?	
Possible conflicts with virtual reference / considerations for time line	

FUTURE PRIORITY	
Audience	
Primary staff involved	
Immediacy	
Awaiting resources?	
Possible conflicts with virtual reference / considerations for time line	

FUTURE PRIORITY	
Audience	
Primary staff involved	
Immediacy	
Awaiting resources?	
Possible conflicts with virtual reference / considerations for time line	

Etc. as needed

➤ If asked, patrons will always recommend longer hours; is that a major purpose for your virtual reference service, or can reference hours remain the same without changing the goals of the implementation?

➤ Is there a conclusive reason to offer reference assistance extended hours, such as a large group of library users in a different time zone or a sizable patron population that works nonstandard shifts?

➤ Is reference service what patrons want in longer library hours, or are they more concerned with checking out books after work?

This scenario illustrates the complexity of staff and patron concerns with a single decision point. Realize that the outcome of every decision will not please everyone. Staff may not always agree. In the example above, some may be eager to work evenings and others may not. Commit to collecting data (facts and feelings) from all affected groups, weighing needs, and discussing options. Be sure that decisions are not seen as always favoring the same group—lest implementation become an issue of patron versus staff, staff versus administration, or staff versus staff.

In chapter 4 we address how to generate interest and work toward consensus within the library. In particular, the section "Ten Ways to Be Convincing" and exercise 4-1 are useful for managing situations where interests diverge.

It Is Not That Difficult, Honestly

You may think that, with an entire book devoted to implementing a virtual reference service, it must be a difficult service to provide. True, the set-up takes consideration and planning, but once it is integrated into a library's reference operations it need not be more difficult than in-person or telephone reference. With good planning and good management, staff find virtual reference to be an easy service to provide to patrons.

As of early 2008, my library is entering its seventh year of offering reference via chat, our fourth with IM. We have offered e-mail reference for at least twenty years. It is routine now. Yes, sometimes we are very busy, but that happens with in-person traffic as well. Sometimes communication is cumbersome because we aren't seeing the patron's screen, but more or less the same awkwardness can also happen with telephone reference. We are used to working around these challenges to good service, just as we are with other challenges we face in a public service environment.

If you, your patrons, or the library staff consider virtual reference service difficult, find the sources of difficulty and work on resolutions. Don't let fear of difficulty be the only reason to not move forward.

Prepare

Prepare for success. This may seem too simple to need stating, but it is a recurring theme throughout this book. Why? Because libraries—consciously or unconsciously—often embark on new projects without clear goals or plans for success. They start projects and do not allocate enough resources.

They start projects as pilots that are too limited in scope to reflect a true implementation. They assign the right tasks to the wrong people, the wrong tasks to the right people, or the wrong tasks to the wrong people. Projects can be undermined by poor planning. They can also be undermined by failure to visualize and prepare for success. If you plan for a weak service, it is doubtful that your virtual reference implementation will be a success.

Your visualization must be realistic. Think about a library as a sports team building a new stadium. Such an undertaking is rarely done because a team is expected to perform poorly. Managers, owners, and fans have faith in the team and plan for a good season and a large crowd. Care is taken in selecting an architect and in lining up supporters so that the project looks appealing and has the resources to be completed. Planning the number of seats takes a look at the projected *success* of a team. Anything else would result in (1) an uninspiringly small facility, (2) a negative impression of the team's prospects, and (3) dampening enthusiasm of benefactors. Everyone likes to be part of a team that, if not winning now, expects to win in the future.

Don't be grandiose, but if you are moving forward, move boldly.

Are You Ready?

Depending on your library's self-assessment of motivations, goals, priorities, and market, it may be time to move forward with virtual reference, or the decision may have been made to table the project and revisit it later. It is also possible that you are still uncertain and feel that virtual reference is a service the library needs to offer right now but one that requires further exploration. Now is the time to decide in which of the following three categories your library falls. Take a deep breath, have a discussion, and decide your next move:

Implementing. At this stage, your library has decided that virtual reference is a priority. You most likely will start a virtual reference service, but there are still questions to consider, such as appropriateness to your audience, and there are still a lot of decisions to be made. I recommend working through this book (with the exception of any parts not applicable to your particular situation), since it is designed as a process.

Still questioning. At this time, your library is not convinced that starting a virtual reference service is the right move. Perhaps there are concerns about staff buy-in or the monetary costs of operation. I advise selectively using the chapters and exercises in this book that address areas where your library needs to know more before making a commitment.

Deferring implementation. At some point (perhaps right now), your library has decided to not move forward with implementation. This may be because of the answers reached during the process of using the exercises and worksheets in this book, or for other reasons. Do not discard this book. You are likely to find yourself in a similar discussion within a few years or even months. Even if the mode of delivery being considered has changed (maybe librarian teleportation instead of chat), the decision-making process in this book remains applicable.

NOTES

1. Lee Raine, "Life Online: Teens, Technology, and the World to Come," 2006, www.pewinternet.org/ppt/Teens%20 and%20technology.pdf.

2. Pew Internet and American Life Project, "Teens and Technology," 2005, www.pewinternet.org/pdfs/PIP_Teens_ Tech_July2005web.pdf (p. 37).

3. Ibid.

4. Pew data memo, www.pewinternet.org/pdfs/PIP_Generations_Memo.pdf (p. 3).

5. M. Kathleen Kern, "Have(n't) We Been Here Before? Lessons from Telephone Reference," *Reference Librarian* 41, no. 85 (2003): 1–17.

6. E-mail communication with Michele Pye, Virtual Library Coordinator, Vancouver Public Library, January 9, 2007.

CHAPTER 3

Who Are We Doing This For?

There are several crucial factors to take into account at the outset of considering a virtual reference service. Assuming that you have decided that your library has solid motivations for considering a new reference offering, it is time for a little deeper analysis of your community and library readiness before committing resources to implementation.

At the top of the list of good reasons for starting a virtual reference service is reaching new audiences and expanding your assistance to existing library users. Every library community has a different population composition. Factors related to your users (as an aggregate group and as individual subgroups) may increase or decrease the viability of virtual reference at your library. These factors also determine which modes of communication will be most effective, if you choose to start a service.

Market Assessment

There are many sources of general data about target audiences. The Pew Internet and American Life reports cited in chapter 2 are a valuable starting point. You can decide to start your service from these general reports and have a successful implementation, but there may be characteristics of your community that make it less (or more) suited for virtual reference than another community. Knowing your community of users also aids greatly in the decisions about which type of virtual service to provide (e-mail, IM, chat, text messaging, etc.), hours of service, and marketing. This entails data gathering, some of which you may choose to do now, and some of which you may choose to do later.

A basic starting point is worksheet 3-1, which is designed to help you analyze the segments of your user population and define known characteristics of your community and their use of the library. The analysis focuses on identification of target audiences and library goals for the service. Most of this worksheet can be done from data already at hand or easily collected, making it an ideal first step. as an example, appendix B contains a market assessment for the fictitious Illumine Library at Erudition College.

Library _____ Date _____

Description of Library

Pleasant Hill Library is an urban public library with a main branch downtown and four smaller neighborhood locations. 80% of population lives within 1.5 miles of a library branch. Patrons represent a range of socioeconomic groups and a growing number of ethnicities, particularly recent South Asian immigrants.

Population Characteristics

AGE GROUP	NUMBER	APPROX. % IM USERS (PEW REPORT 2005)	APPROX. % E-MAIL USERS (PEW REPORT 2005)	NUMBER OF CARD HOLDERS
Total population				
6–12				
13–18				
19–25				
. . .				
Over 55				

5-year trends in circulation (may wish to break down into type of material: children's, YA, adult, media, course reserves, etc.)

5-year trends in reference inquiries (by type of communication, if known)

Other usage data (gate counts, computer usage, database usage)

Current programs for specific populations and attendance

Assessment

Conclusions

Surveys and Focus Groups

It is possible to determine target audiences and need from an evaluation based on data that you, mostly likely, already have about your user population. Some libraries go further in their exploration of user preferences before they implement a new service. There are several good reasons to do this, and as with most undertakings also a couple of reasons to be cautious.

Below I review several examples of ways to collect information from your users about their preferences for communication and their information habits. These are merely overviews, but many detailed resources about conducting surveys and focus groups are also available. An excellent source, which I also recommend when you start considering marketing strategies, is Fisher and Pride's *Blueprint for Your Library Marketing Plan.*[1]

Surveys

A familiar way to collect information from your users is a survey. The Web has made the distribution and collection of surveys easy. Depending on what you want to collect, you may place the survey form online for anyone to take, send a notice containing the survey URL to selected people, or give the survey to your patrons at the end of a virtual reference interaction.

When designing your survey, keep it short and keep it focused. People have better tolerance for a short survey and are more likely to complete all of the questions. Focusing on issues directly related to your current project (virtual reference) will aid you when you process the data. Collect only the information you think you will use, not all of the data about which you are curious.

Take advantage of any data that may be automatically collected by the survey software but be cognizant of privacy issues. For instance, it may be useful to know if a patron is answering from an in-library computer or from outside the library, but who will see this data? Is there a way to merely sort by library IP and nonlibrary IP without viewing the full-IP address? Your library IT department may be helpful in providing ways to process the data while maintaining user anonymity.

Finally, remember that multiple choice, yes/no, and ranking questions are far easier to process than open-ended questions, and survey software often includes the capability to manipulate the data. The impact on the survey taker is lighter as well, since these questions take less time to answer. On the other hand, open-ended questions allow users to answer with their own voice and can provide answers that go beyond what the survey designer conceptualized. Balance these issues in deciding on the type of response needed and the design of the questions.

There are many resources to help your library with writing and administering a survey. Two useful books are *How to Conduct Surveys: A Step-by-Step Guide* and *Survey Research: The Basics*, but there are many books and websites devoted to the basics of writing and conducting a survey.[2]

Focus Groups

The most open-ended and personal way to collect information is through focus groups. A good focus group is not a free-for-all; it is focused and led by a facilitator who can keep the discussion on track without stifling individual voices.[3] You may choose to seek someone with experience in focus groups to assist your library in the planning and execution. There are numerous library consultants, but members of your town or campus community may also have these skills to lend.

Key considerations with focus groups are planning questions that will generate discussion, capturing the discussion, and collecting a group of willing participants. As with survey questions, what is asked should be focused but not leading. In recording the discussion, decide what will be comfortable for you users, maintain the standards of privacy your institution requires, and also provide an adequate transcript. Videotaping may be permissible at your library and is the most complete documentation, if the technology is set up correctly. It may, however, make your participants self-conscious (and it is necessary that they know they are being recorded). There are similar considerations with audio recordings. Typed transcription is less intrusive but also less complete. Consult a resource on focus groups (and your campus research board or town legal counsel) to determine how best to record the proceedings.

What to Not Ask Patrons, and Why

Patron data, whether from surveys or focus groups, may well be interesting—but it may not be that reliable. Patrons may answer that they want or would use services even though they are unfamiliar with the technology or do not understand the terminology used by the library. Something new may seem like a good idea just because it is new, or its very unfamiliarity may cause assumptions about its utility. Designing your questions to ask what methods of communication patrons use in their daily lives in addition to what they would use to ask questions of the library may help you better assess their answers. You might consider not asking anything about library preferences at all and instead concentrate on communication and information habits.

There also may be a disconnect between what patrons think they will use (or do use) and what they actually use. This is known to be true of surveys that ask patrons if they use electronic library resources. Many patrons do not identify online information from the library as different from other online information. Supplemental information, such as staff observations of IM use within the library, may aid in determining the accuracy of answers.

Keep in mind that, no matter how much information you collect, it may not prove to be a match with experience once a service is implemented. This cuts in both directions: patrons may use less or more than you expect from the results of your investigations. For this reason, I recommend assessing your user population, but knowing when to stop. It may be desirable to save surveys and focus groups for a different stage of the decision-making process, such as when planning marketing or assessing the outcomes of your service.

Library Goals

Finding the Target Audience

Just as it is important to know your market for virtual reference, it is essential to determine the library's goals for starting a virtual reference service. The library has reasons for starting the service, so what are the desired outcomes? Who does the library wish to use the service?

These are not trivial questions. If you answer "everyone," that is okay, but really think about it; are there preferred groups the library wishes to reach? How do the library's goals match with the market assessment? Where is there overlap? Where is there disconnect? For some libraries, the teen market and homework assistance may be the primary focus of virtual reference service; for others, this is a market they may choose to exclude. These are differences in library goals; in most public library communities, teens show up as a strong potential audience on a market assessment, but not all libraries have teens as the intended users.

Colleges may extend reference service to their alumni (limited, often by the online resources available to alumni), but this is generally not the main group these libraries seek to serve with their virtual reference services. A large response to the service by alumni does not represent a failure of the service, but if it is out of proportion to the primary intended user group of currently enrolled students, then the library has a popular service that has not met its goals.

To match library goals to target audience, it may be useful to think in terms of primary, ancillary, and excluded groups of users. Policy issues related to serving various groups are addressed in chapter 5. At this point, though, you should think about what your library hopes to achieve by starting a new service. Table 3-1 is a way to keep track of the possible audiences for virtual reference service, their likelihood of being users, and the library's goals in relation to this population. Use this information to help determine if your goals match your potential users, and save it to inform your policies, marketing, and assessment activities.

In the examples in table 3-1, the 11–13 age group is a large (public library) population with robust IM activity, but it is not at the center of the library's virtual reference goals (nor are they excluded). The 26–35 group is the one the library most hopes to reach. This group uses e-mail actively, and IM has a foothold but is not pervasive. An e-mail-only service might reach this group and basically exclude the preteens. This is good information to have on hand, presented clearly by bringing together the market assessment with the library's goals.

The faculty group (assuming a higher-education setting) ranks high on the library's desired list for users of virtual reference, but they are not active users of IM. The library may then opt to reach the faculty via an e-mail reference service, or focus efforts on reaching the undergraduates who rate strongly in the market assessments and are the primary target group. Any faculty that use the IM

TABLE 3-1   DEFINING YOUR AUDIENCE

Group	Market assessment (IM)	Market assessment (e-mail)	Library target audience
11–13	4	1	3
26–35	3	4	5
. . .	. . .	. . .	. . .
Faculty	1	4	4
Undergrad students	5	3	5

Note: 1–5 scale where 5 is strongest and 1 is weakest.

service are most welcome, but the library must decide if it is important to design the service for them or to concentrate, at least initially, on its primary target group and a more certain market for IM service.

Matching the Who, What, and Why

The most important question to ask when deciding if this is the right time for your library to start a new (or change an existing) virtual reference service is, What do you want to achieve? The answer to this fundamental question will lead in the choice of target audience, development of policies, and choice of software. It may impact how and with whom you staff.

Exercise 3-1 is an individual exercise to initiate thinking about goals and expectation. The managers of the virtual reference service should certainly use this exercise, but it may be useful to give to everyone involved in planning and providing the service. It is not an exercise to be collected and evaluated—just a place for people to write down initial ideas and collect their thoughts before being asked to participate.

NOTES

1. Patricia H. Fisher and Marseille M. Pride, *Blueprint for Your Library Marketing Plan: A Guide to Help You Survive and Thrive* (Chicago: American Library Association, 2005).
2. Arlene Fink, *How to Conduct Surveys: A Step-by-Step Guide,* 2nd ed. (Thousand Oaks, CA: Sage, 1998). Keith F. Punch, *Survey Research: The Basics* (London: Sage, 2003).
3. Claudia Puchta and Jonathan Potter, *Focus Group Practice* (London: Sage, 2004).

Reflections on Purpose and Goals

Your library is planning to implement virtual reference. What type of service will you have? Which communication tools are you considering (chat, e-mail, IM, etc.)?

Consider the following questions. This is the start of developing a philosophy of service for virtual reference and the underpinnings for a service policy. This is a reflection piece for you; you should keep your answers in mind during the rest of the planning process, although it is fine if your responses change.

- ➤ Who would be the target audience(s) for this service?
- ➤ Who do you expect will make the most use of the service?
- ➤ What types of questions might these patrons ask through the service?
- ➤ What do you want the service to achieve?
- ➤ What are the benefits to the patron?
- ➤ Are there benefits for the library?

And to think about later . . . how will the answers to these questions affect the other decision points?

CHAPTER 4

Buy-in

GAINING COMMITMENT AND SUPPORT

The VR Guidelines state that there should be a commitment to virtual reference from all levels of a library's organization before a service is implemented. Without adequate support, any undertaking is set up for failure, and virtual reference is no exception, so commitment is necessary early in the process of implementation. There are two types of support: support for the concept and support with resources. In this chapter we focus on obtaining support for the concept of virtual reference, since this is typically a prerequisite to a commitment of money, staff, and other resources.

Some virtual reference initiatives start as grassroots efforts from frontline library staff. Others are driven by library administration. Both origin points can lead to viable services, but buy-in from all levels of the organization is necessary for success.

Buy-in is often easier said than achieved. The pressing question is how to move those reluctant people, at whatever level of the organization, from hesitancy (or even hostility) to acceptance and perhaps enthusiasm.

Achieving Commitment

There are a variety of people from whom commitment to virtual reference is needed before a successful implementation can truly begin. Except in the smallest of libraries, virtual reference is a group effort. The larger and more complex the organization, the more people are likely to be involved, in some measure, with the virtual reference service. A key step is identifying who in the organization has a role in the implementation process. Support from administration is necessary to provide stable funding and continuance of virtual reference beyond the pilot project stage. Commitment from staff providing the service is needed to ensure quality of service and to avoid burnout or resentment. These two groups are fairly obvious, but what about the library's information technology staff? Do the circulation desk staff have a role? What about librarians involved in collecting materials who do not provide frontline service? Some people may have roles that are small in terms of time and effort but nonetheless central to the process. Some people may provide support through influence, others through tangibles such as budget and technical support.

Knowing Who Needs to Be Involved

You may have people clamoring to be involved with virtual reference, or you may need to make individual invitations and meet with people one-on-one to explain their crucial role. Whatever the situation at your library, you need to know what different personnel have to offer to the implementation and continued success of this new service. It is more important to have up-front support from some groups (like administration) than others (collections staff), but most often people appreciate being consulted and feeling like they know what is going on, even when they are not key decision makers.

Administration

The people at the top of library management generally control the money. Commitment from them is vital at this most basic level, for it underpins other resources such as software, equipment, and perhaps even staff. Virtual reference service does have costs, and we explore budgeting in chapter 9. For now, just remember that you cannot provide something for nothing and that financial commitment is necessary.

Administrators also set priorities for the library. Beyond money, their support can garner interest from others within, and outside, the library. It can motivate a reluctant IT department or a reticent reference librarian to lend their skills to virtual reference. The director of the library is an important link with external groups such as campus administration, donors, and civic groups. A good word from the director can result in increased traffic to the library's virtual reference service, funding, or collaborations. A library administration may be able to find opportunities or open doors, such as arranging for seniors in the advertising program to design marketing materials or obtaining an invitation for the virtual reference coordinator to speak before the local chamber of commerce.

Reference Staff

These people are the face (so to speak) of the virtual reference service. It is their voice that comes through the typed words of an instant message or e-mail. Their enthusiasm, or lack thereof, is evident in the service they provide. Although lack of visual cues and tone of voice may hide a bored look or a frustrated tone of voice, negativity can seep through in virtual communications. Even when it is not the intent of the librarian to display his attitude toward the service, his underlying feelings may be exhibited—by virtual equivalents of pointing (overly short e-mails, links sent though chat with no explanation), lack of interest (lengthy pauses without communication, insufficient reference interview), and terse word choice.

Conversely, an enthusiastic staff member will actively promote the service by telling patrons about it. It might be promoted during an instruction session or recommended to a student leaving for spring break. At my library, the staff who are most happy with our virtual reference service are likely to mention it to telephone patrons and even to hand out the Ask a Librarian business cards to in-person patrons. They invite the patron to return to ask questions using any type of communication, and the personal way they promote virtual reference creates interest from the patron.

Reference staff also have plentiful experience to bring to the planning of the virtual reference service. They understand the library's patrons and the best ways to reach out to them. They know what types of questions are asked and can recommend training that might be needed to supplement training on the virtual reference software. Frequently, reference staff have other responsibilities, such as outreach to specific campus departments or planning of library programming, that make them uniquely suited to promoting the service. Staff also have personal skills and interests that they may offer to the benefit of the library if they are excited about the service. You may find someone with radio experience to record a commercial or someone willing to work a late-night or weekend shift.

Of course, the most important reason to have the support of reference staff is the desire to have dedicated and happy people working at the library. Starting a virtual reference service without buy-in from the frontline reference staff is a sure path to burnout.

Information Technology Staff

Depending on the specifics of your implementation, the library's IT staff may be responsible for all of the technical support of your service, or their involvement may be small. But because virtual reference is a computer-supported service, they will be involved in one way or another. It is a good idea to get them on board early.

Librarians do not always realize what IT has to offer to projects beyond supporting whatever it is the rest of the library staff determine is needed. Since they are often overlooked when it comes to creating work teams, an "us versus them" mentality can develop between IT and librarians. Avoid this pattern. Acknowledge that there are technical needs of this service and that they will have an impact on the IT staff. Also know that the IT staff will have ready answers to some questions that may arise when choosing software. Do you know what server platforms your library uses? Do you know how much staff time it will take each year to host virtual reference software on your library's servers? Would it be more cost effective to pay the vendor to host, or to host locally?

Compatibility with existing systems and configurations is another issue that can get lost when there is a gap between public services and IT. If your virtual reference system uses pop-up windows, the virtual reference website must be permanently set as a trusted site on your in-library workstations. If Java is needed, do your library computers support the correct version? IT policy can also intersect with virtual reference services. When promoting an IM service, consider if library IT policy allows the use of IM on the public computers. A surprising number of people contact a librarian via IM from computers within the library. It would be awkward to be blocking in-library patrons from your service.

The IT staff can also provide information about your users you may be unaware of. They may be tracking the operating systems used by visitors to the library's website, for instance. They may also know what percentage of patrons use online library resources from within the library and from outside the library. If you are on a college campus, they may also know, through collecting IP ranges, what percentage are on campus, off campus, in dormitories, or in offices and laboratories. They are

probably recording time of day people visit the library's website and even more specifically when they are using e-journals, the library's online catalog, and the like. This is all data that can help you define the service. So, find an interested member of the IT staff to be on the implementation committee or, at the very least, be a willing and ready resource for questions that arise.

Access Services

Circulation and interlibrary lending personnel are groups which, like IT, are often outside the perception of reference librarians except when there is an immediate and pressing need for their involvement. How direct their role will be in your virtual reference service depends a lot on your organization, but here are some things to consider.

Does it make sense for access services to have a public face through virtual reference? Within the library, there may be separate circulation and reference service desks. Patrons may be used to this physical set-up, but their expectations from a virtual service may not be the same, and they may ask any library-related question of the virtual service. How many telephone calls are transferred between the reference desk and the circulation desk?

If this is not a good option for your library, will the reference staff handle basic circulation questions and transactions through the virtual reference service or will patrons be directed to call the appropriate office? Will circulation inquiries be accepted through e-mail but not, perhaps, through chat? These are issues to be decided with the access services department. An important question here is whether the software used ensures adequate confidentiality of the patron information often needed for circulation and interlibrary loan. The head of access services should know what these are and the best ways to handle this data. Access services are best situated to provide training for the reference staff in this area.

Collections and Cataloging

Much like access services, collections and cataloging staff do not frequently provide direct reference services to patrons, except in small libraries where the librarians have diverse roles. Virtual reference may create opportunities for staff who wish for some public contact to expand their experiences. Depending on your staffing model, you may find that the extra hands are needed, and this can be mutually beneficial. On the other hand, many technical services staff enjoy the lack of direct patron contact. Support from technical services does not need to be in the hands-on day-to-day of working with patrons via virtual reference.

Virtual reference service takes library resources. It is good for all of the library staff to understand the purpose and goals of the service. At my library, we occasionally field a question from a staff member outside the reference department; though they work at the library, their specialization is elsewhere and they should feel welcome to "ask a librarian." In extended organizations, it can also be useful for staff to know that the virtual reference service can assist them with finding internal library documents or staff web pages.

Online collections go hand-in-hand with virtual reference. One of the driving reasons for virtual reference is patrons' use of electronic resources. If reference staff are not involved in purchasing decisions for electronic resources, coordination with these librarians is essential. Virtual reference

may increase the use of all of your online resources, or of specific titles if the service is promoted to a particular class or reference staff encourage patrons in the use of new resources. Thus, attention to usage statistics for electronic resources is important, particularly for resources that are limited to a set number of concurrent users rather than offering unlimited access.

Virtual reference interactions may lead you to discover needed resources. Print titles remain important to library collections and are used by virtual reference librarians, but online titles receive more use since patrons can be directed to use these titles themselves, and for factual information it is easier to copy and paste than to type. Electronic databases and reference sources also allow decentralized staffing: a librarian can answer virtual reference questions with the same accuracy from home, office, or reference desk, and libraries in a large system or members of a consortium may all have access to the same titles. Although it is unrealistic to predict the demise of the book, there has been a substantial shift toward electronic publishing in reference sources and journal indexing and abstracting. Collections librarians are quite aware of these changes, but communication between acquisitions and public services is important, especially where budgets are tight and titles are unlikely to be duplicated across formats.

Boards, Friends, and Other Affiliated Groups

Outreach, outreach, outreach. Groups affiliated with the library but not composed of library employees are in a unique position to bring your message to nonlibrarians. They have workplaces outside the library with colleagues who might use a new virtual reference service. They may be part of different civic organizations and have different circles of friends. They are already supporters of the library, so get them interested in talking about this particular service.

They are also much more representative of your general user population than are library employees. They don't, obviously, reflect the nonuser, but they are more typical library users than people who spend their work lives in the library. They may tell you how they would (or wouldn't) use e-mail or chat to contact the library. Their questions about the service will also help you recognize any ambiguities about the service policies or description.

Library boards and Friends groups also contribute in various ways to the library budget and can help set priorities through monetary support of initiatives. You might be bold and ask for this to be an item in a fundraising campaign, or maybe the idea of virtual reference will be so inspiring that someone else will suggest it.

How to Make Support Happen

Now that you know who should be involved and why, how do you introduce the idea of implementing virtual reference or expanding your service to include new communications media? You may have an organization in which everyone is enthusiastic about new initiatives. Perhaps virtual reference has been a topic of discussion for some time already. In these cases, starting a discussion about the new service is easy. You may even move fairly quickly through the early parts of the implementation (such as audience and policies) if this groundwork is already in place.

It may be, however, that virtual reference—or a particular aspect of virtual reference—is a new idea to your institution or one that is contested. It is likely that many people will be enthusiastic, but there are usually a few people with reservations. See this as an opportunity to create interest and to answer the difficult questions. The effort and reflection needed to generate support can result in a more robust service than one that is confronted with few questions. For an example of how one library achieved a broad base of support to start a virtual reference service in a short amount of time, read the Library Field Report from Alex Sonsteby at Concordia College.

As the Concordia example shows, there is no reason to fear people with questions or concerns. Use them as an advantage, and an opportunity, to really use the processes in this book (and your own knowledge and skills) to be thorough in your planning.

Ten Ways to Be Convincing

At the very beginning of the implementation process, before the decision to implement has even been agreed upon, lay out the reasons and know how to build a team of supporters across the organization. Here are a few basic steps for achieving buy-in:

Be organized. A well-managed implementation project can do its own work to convince people of the viability of virtual reference. Poor project planning runs the risk of turning off staff who would otherwise be supporters.

Prepare in advance. You know the people at your library and what they would like to know. Anticipate questions and be prepared with answers and discussion points. In some organizations readings in advance of meetings are appreciated; at others the hands-on demo and discussion are the best approach, with suggested (and selective) readings provided as a follow-up.

Select your evidence. What did you read, hear, or observe that convinced you to initiate a virtual reference service? Share this information with others in your library who may want it. See the Library Field Report in this chapter for an example of successful sharing of evidence. Selection is more important than volume. A few well-chosen pieces of reading are more persuasive than a three-inch binder of articles: perhaps some relevant data from the Pew Internet and American Life reports or other surveys, a couple of case studies or research articles about implementations that include some assessment data, and a well-written column or two.

Know who needs to know what. This is not about hiding information, but the library's IT staff needs to know different things and have different questions than do the librarians who staff the service. Not everyone needs to be present at every meeting. Who is involved in planning and how you arrange meetings depend on the size and structure of your organization.

Listen to concerns. Change can be uncomfortable and a little scary. People need space to voice their opinions. More important, concerns may help guide decisions by bringing up issues that may otherwise have been overlooked or unforeseen.

Converse. Learn the why, not just the what, from reluctant participants. Ask for possible solutions or scenarios that would ameliorate the concern. For example, if someone is concerned about an increased workload, discussion may reveal a creative staffing solution.

Bring in someone from outside. Quite a few libraries have implemented virtual reference. Find a librarian or staff member at a library with a successful service to lead a formal workshop or informal discussion at your library. An outsider can sometimes do a lot by being independent of your organizational dynamics.

Be clear and be definite. Wishy-washy is not convincing. If a concern is voiced to which the implementation team does not have an answer, regroup and research; don't muddle through.

Ease into it. Framing the initial implementation as a pilot confirms that there is the flexibility to change or discontinue the service at the end of the pilot. A pilot phase may also be somewhat (but not dramatically) smaller in terms of hours or service or number of people involved, sidestepping the most reluctant players until there is proof of concept.

Know when to let go. Some staff may never be convinced—possibly because of something specific to virtual reference, possibly as an ingrained personality trait. Avoid unproductive arguing, for this can bring the rest of the group down (see chapter 8 for a discussion of reluctant reference staffers). Someone wise once told me, "You cannot argue with personal experience." You can provide examples of different experiences, but you will never be able to convince a person that his experience is wrong. Take note of the person's concerns so that they can be addressed later. Some of them may become the initial questions for your assessment of the service.

Buy-in is generally not a big hurdle; there are likely many people in your library supportive and enthusiastic about virtual reference. There may be a few who are uncertain. If you feel that it is you against the world, it may be prudent to reassess whether this is the time for virtual reference at your library. More likely there will be many questions, many supporters, and a little reluctance that must be faced. It is possible that the person asking the most questions will become the biggest supporter.

Starting the Conversation

Discussions start with listening. Exercise 4-1 encourages staff to share their perceptions about virtual reference. There may be excitement. There may be fear. There should be questions and concerns. All of these feelings can coexist in the same person, and certainly within the same staff.

It is best if this exercise is done in an open environment where everyone shares their opinions and their own feelings. I have written the exercise in this manner. You may, of course, modify the instructions to fit your group dynamics. Make sure the discussion is captured. Flipcharts or moveable whitewalls are great for this, since everyone can see the discussion mapped as it happens and then the notes can be taken away to be typed up. This is an important part of the follow-up. Set a time limit for the sharing part of the exercise. My recommendation for a group of six or seven people is thirty minutes.

Alternative Instructions

Inviting a facilitator who is perceived as neutral is one way to encourage openness. Another way to be sure that everyone participates is a round-robin style of sharing where people take turns reading their lists. This can help avoid some voices dominating while others are silent, but it may also make

Concordia College's Road to Instant Messaging

The Carl B. Ylvisaker Library serves Concordia College, a small, private, residential liberal arts college located in Moorhead, Minnesota. The college provides undergraduate education to approximately 2,800 students and supports a nascent graduate program in nursing. The library's collections are enhanced through strong relationships with Minnesota State University, Moorhead, and North Dakota State University in Fargo, North Dakota.

Having come from an institution that strongly supports virtual reference services through instant messaging, I wanted to explore the possibility of the library providing such services to the Concordia community.

I introduced my colleagues to the idea by e-mailing them articles about the benefits and lows costs of IM reference. Eventually, we started to discuss the matter at our weekly meetings. There was some initial skepticism that such a service would even be used, so I leaned on statistics about IM usage (e.g., from the Pew Internet and American Life Project) and my own experiences in my previous position. Eventually three questions emerged: (1) Were IM reference questions less important than in-person questions? (2) How would the service be staffed? (3) How does IM even work?

To address the first question, I shared the ALA Code of Ethics, which reminds us librarians that we do not judge our users' questions or the means they seek information but instead provide the "highest level of service to all library users" and "courteous responses to all requests."

I approached the second question by describing my two years of experience as a graduate assistant in the reference library at the University of Illinois. The University of Illinois library staffed IM from the desk, and staffing needs remained fairly constant even as IM usage increased. I also explained mechanisms we used to prioritize questions and maintain high-quality service through busy periods.

Since I was the only librarian at Concordia who had ever used IM, we all installed an IM client on our computers and practiced communicating with each other for several weeks to increase our comfort level. Soon my colleagues said that they felt like they were "hip" and "cool" and that we were helping to bring the library into the "twenty-first century."

After addressing these concerns, the Concordia library faculty decided to entertain a proposal for IM reference. The reference team used RUSA's VR Guidelines as a model. I then developed and taught a three-hour IM reference training program for the librarians before we went live.

Concordia's IM service is staffed by the reference librarian working the reference desk during the desk's open hours. So far, service has been light (thirty-nice IM questions during spring semester), so it will be the focus of a fall marketing campaign.

Alec Sonsteby, Instruction/Reference Librarian, Concordia College, Moorhead, Minnesota people feel pressured. You could choose to have people submit their responses to a facilitator to compile. This provides more anonymity, which may encourage more openness, but it also allows people to avoid ownership of their opinions; therefore, it is my least recommended approach to this type of sharing activity.

For clarity, if you are altering the instructions, be sure to type up a new exercise rather than photocopying the one provided here and verbally communicate changes. This avoids confusion.

Conversation Follow-up

Not all of the issues—be they concerns, questions, or enthusiastically offered ideas—can be addressed immediately. During the communication on views of virtual reference, some dialogue between people will occur. Do not try to answer everything immediately. There is a difference between being prepared and being controlling; realize and convey that this is a process, and that some decisions will be addressed at a later time.

Synthesize the notes from the discussion into a coherent document. Group the comments by themes that emerge (e.g., communication, staffing, technology, competing needs). Place concerns, questions to be addressed later, and creative ideas in subcategories. Some items will be listed by more than one person but stated in different ways; these can be combined. The intent is an easily read record of issues specific to the staff and culture of your library that you can refer to during the decision-making process.

Starting the Conversation

Your perceptions as an individual are important. Out of these come ideas for direction and issues to be addressed by the library. You will be asked to share your thoughts on virtual reference services with the rest of the group. Everyone's statements will be recorded at the front of the room and kept for later referral. To allow everyone time to speak their piece, in-depth discussion may be held for later.

There are no restrictions: concerns, questions, personal experiences, and examples are all welcome. Concentrate on your own opinions.

There will be twenty minutes allotted for this exercise.

The space below is provided if you want to collect your thoughts in writing before sharing them with the group.

CHAPTER 5

Policies

SETTING EXPECTATIONS OF WHO, WHEN, AND WHAT

P olicies don't just exist; they relate to a more fundamental concept of what the library wants to achieve. Writing a policy is, in part, about setting expectations. Your policy communicates to patrons what they can expect from your virtual reference service. It should let patrons know who may use the service, when they can expect assistance, and what questions your service will answer. Actual content of service policies varies by library; there is no single model policy for virtual reference, just as there is no uniform policy for in-person reference. There are, however, elements that every policy should contain and some best practices for writing a policy.

Start Here: Why?

The best virtual reference policies are grounded in a shared philosophy of service. This is really true of any reference, circulation, or other public service policy. They stem from thoughtful consideration of what reference service means at your institution. By addressing the question of service philosophy, staff know why a policy is written as it is and are better able to offer a consistently uniform (and high) level of service.

There is no uniform philosophy about reference service that fits all libraries. Although we all mean to offer excellent service, just what "excellence of service" means varies from library to library. For a public library, service excellence may mean assisting all who walk through the doors to find the information they need. For an academic library, it may be assisting researchers at all levels to search for information and evaluate available resources, and it may be teaching them to be independent, information literate researchers. Special libraries may define appropriate service as providing information only to their clientele and even extend this to anticipating their information needs to provide information before it is requested.

Your library's philosophy of service may become a visible part of your virtual reference policy. Often, it is the introduction to a more detailed policy statement. For example: "The reference service of the University of ZYX assists the students, faculty, and staff with their research questions. As an academic institution, it is our mission to educate researchers in locating and evaluating information and enable them to conduct better research now and in the future." The policy statement would then continue to encompass specifics of the service, such as what is available to nonaffiliated users and the other areas covered in this chapter. A staff member would know if an encounter with a patron met this service philosophy by reflecting on whether she had not only helped the person find information but increased the patron's understanding of information and research.

Before moving into the area of policy specifics, divide into small groups (five people or fewer) and discuss the reference service philosophy at your library; this is exercise 5-1. As a short conversation, this might be a good coffee break exercise. It is followed nicely by exercise 5-2, which applies service philosophies to concrete policies.

Outcomes of exercise 5-1:

➤ Reminder to everyone that virtual reference is grounded in our professional philosophy of service
➤ Identification of the characteristics of the institutional philosophy of service

Who

Since virtual reference services are not behind physical walls, they appear to be open to the world, and it is common for libraries to state in their policies that their virtual reference service is limited to patrons defined by a particular geography (a city or county) or membership within a particular group (e.g., students at a specific university). It is important that users know that they can "ask a librarian." Unaffiliated users may choose to come in and ask questions anyway (see "Scope and Enforcement," below), but parameters have been set and announced.

Some libraries require users to log in with their library ID, ZIP code, or other identification to ensure that all users of the virtual reference service are their affiliates. Corporate libraries are likely to place their virtual reference services on the company intranet, an area accessible only to the employees. If a library has a proxy server or other means of authenticating user access to its subscription databases, this may be an option for restricting access to the Ask a Librarian services. Access measures this limiting are not universally popular, and publicly funded libraries in particular may find this a difficult policy to justify.

Verification of Patron Affiliation

Libraries that require log-ins or verification of affiliation effectively bar nonaffiliates from inquiring about their collections and their community. Nonaffiliated users who may have questions (perhaps questions than can be answered only by that library, like policy or holdings questions) can contact the library in other ways such as via telephone. But this may not be the best marketing if a library is seeking to reach out to nonusers. Imagine not being able to ask about how to obtain a library card because the virtual reference service requires you to use a library card to log in to the service. A few public libraries require users to provide a library ID to ask questions through their virtual services, but it is more common to ask only for a ZIP code, which does not really verify user status (since it is easy to give a false code) but may discourage some nonaffiliated users. An advantage of

Coffee Break Discussion
of Service Philosophy

This is natural follow-up to previous exercises about the purpose of the virtual reference service. Over coffee or lunch, talk about your philosophy of service. Why do we help our patrons? What is the goal of reference service in general? What do we expect to be the outcomes of our interactions with patrons?

If your group is large, mingle with both close colleagues and those you don't know as well.

The discussion may progress into more specifics such as who we serve, the nature and detail of our assistance, and any other areas that are part of a broad understanding of what it means to be a reference librarian and offer reference service at our library. This may well be fun and energizing, since we are talking about what is core to our library's mission.

this approach is that it leaves access open to residents who have not yet become cardholding library users but may be attracted by the virtual reference.

Private academic libraries are most likely to require users to verify their affiliation, whereas publicly funded academic libraries are more bound to keep the virtual reference service open to all people of the state. It is problematic for libraries that are federal depositories to implement restricted access, since this contradicts the creed of open access to government information.

When users are asked to provide identifying information such as library ID, privacy is also a concern. Although this information can be separated from the patron's questions in library logs, discuss with your software vendor the extent of the software privacy mechanisms. The chat software may be secure enough that there is never anything connecting the patron information to the question. If you are hosting the software on your library's servers, or the patron ID appears on the librarian's computer screen (even if it is not saved by the software), then you should also talk with your library IT staff about what shadows may remain of patron identifying information.

Although requiring verification of patron affiliation may seem an easy way to limit the service to the intended users, it is in fact complicated. It is imperative that you make sure your verification policy is consistent with other library policies and that there are not unintended consequences.

Priority

One of the most frequent questions I am asked when I consult with libraries starting a chat or IM service is how they should prioritize patrons when there is more than one question. Multiple simultaneous questions are more an issue for libraries that staff virtual reference from the public service desk, but it is also entirely possible to have more than one virtual patron at a time. I always ask, in turn, what these libraries do now when they have multiple reference patrons. For some libraries, traffic is slow enough at the reference desk that this never happens, but for many it does.

Most libraries answer the telephone and walk-up patrons from the same location. I doubt that more than a few of those libraries have set rules that are either first-come/first-served or in-person takes priority over telephone. This type of rigidity is not practical, nor is it polite. We are not banks; we do not queue with a rope and tell people when they can approach the desk. Our patrons expect to be noticed, whether we are helping another patron or not. The in-person patron does not expect us to ignore the ringing phone and might even be appalled if we did so; it would turn them away from calling us themselves.

So what about the virtual patron? My advice is to pick up the incoming message as if it were a ringing telephone. Ask the patron to hold if you need to. Inform her that you are assisting another patron; she will likely assume it is another virtual patron. Even better, first find out what her inquiry is, and if it is something easier to deal with than the question you already have in process, answer it and then return to your first patron. Keep your language with both patrons positive. "Do you mind waiting a minute while I help this patron? It should be quick and then I can give your question more time." Staggering questions also works. Move one patron to a point where he is looking at resources, help the second patron, and then return to the first for follow-up or additional assistance. Chapter 7, on communication, has more detail about getting back to chat and IM patrons through e-mail.

Here, I will just mention that e-mail is better used as an exception and not as a way to handle simultaneous patrons.

Some libraries set priority by type of patron. This may be the case in special libraries, where someone higher in the organization receives more immediate attention. Even in my academic library, where students and faculty are on equal status for service, if the provost's office calls or e-mails (as far as I know, they have never used our chat service), this question is given priority for completion. Your prioritization for virtual reference questions should follow the same written policies and unwritten practices as for in-person and telephone patrons. If prioritization is based on predetermined criteria such as patron type or first-come/first-served, this should be mentioned in your patron policy. If the prioritization is more ad hoc and situational, then a public statement about this is not necessary. Some libraries state on their websites simply that there may be a wait if multiple patrons are being assisted.

It is not always necessary to post a policy statement about how you set priority. Consider whether your policy is something patrons need to know in order to understand the assistance they receive, such as with a first-in/first-out policy. If not, what you have are really just guidelines for your staff, and patrons do not need to see them.

What

If users can ask anything, let them know that they can. If the service is intended for specific types of questions or if some types of questions are prohibited, this is an important policy to communicate. Some public libraries do not answer "homework help" questions from K–12 students; for other libraries this is a specific service offered through virtual reference. It was once common for libraries to specify that virtual reference was intended to answer *quick* or *factual* ready-reference questions but was not available for research assistance. This policy has, for the most part, fallen out of favor, at least among academic libraries. Libraries simply do not receive many ready-reference questions now that quick, factual information needs are easily met by searching the open Web. Thus, most policies now meet the reality that patrons desire to ask research questions using virtual reference.

In drafting a policy about what questions will be addressed, it is important to keep in mind the types of questions your patrons are likely to want answered. This is, after all, a service, and the point is to meet patron's information needs. It is good to keep in mind that patrons are likely to want to ask the same types of questions via virtual reference that they ask in person or via telephone. A study of questions asked in person, via e-mail, and via chat reference at Penn State University found a higher percentage of reference questions asked online and a higher percentage of directional and policy questions asked in person. Most interesting is that a far greater percentage of strategy-based questions (where to start research, how to use databases) were asked online versus in person.[1] There will be some variation in patron preference for what is asked through which medium because some modes of communication lend themselves to certain types of questions more than others— for example, questions about remote access to databases are unlikely to be asked at the in-person reference desk—but in the larger picture, patron needs are consistent regardless of their physical location or choice of communication medium.

When

E-mail

Patrons can ask questions, virtually, any time. E-mail allows them to send inquiries when all of the library's staff are at home asleep or on holiday. The library's policy should state how quickly e-mail will be answered, generally in terms of business days. Aiming a little broad on the time estimation ensures that the library always exceeds expectations, but don't set your stated e-mail response time so long that it discourages users. If it will take two business days to reply to patron e-mail, this may prevent people from using your service, so don't set the estimate this long unless that is really the best you can do. The time needed to respond does depend on the type of library and the type of question. A historical society might have a longer response turnaround than an academic library because of the nature, for instance, of genealogical research. A good practice, if the library's typical response time is more than half a day, is to send an auto-reply that the patron's message has been received and restate the expected response time. A more personal approach is to triage each e-mail individually, answering those that take less than ten minutes and sending brief messages to the other patrons with an estimated response time customized to the question being asked and the number of pending questions awaiting response.

Chat and IM

For synchronous virtual reference, *when* is largely a matter of communicating the hours a patron can expect to talk with a librarian. Another *when* consideration may be alerting patrons that they could be asked to hold if the service is busy.

If the chat or IM service operates fewer hours than in-person or telephone reference, the virtual reference policy should alert patrons that they can ask questions through different channels when the virtual reference service is closed. If the service is staffed after-hours by a contracted service or is part of a cooperative, it is polite to let patrons know when the local librarians are staffing but that they can ask questions any time the service is open.

Placement of Policy

Do not bury the use policy so deeply that it takes a bloodhound to find it. This is a public document. The policy may be broken up into segments and placed in strategically appropriate locations. For instance, place hours in one location and who staffs the service in another. Embedding concisely worded policies within the service's web page increases the likelihood that some of it will be read. A link to the policy as a single, more intricately worded document may be provided for the truly curious or for librarians who stop by to check out your service. It is also useful for those (rare, we hope) times when a policy document is needed to back up a practice.

Some libraries make the use policy a click-through so that all users see it before they ask a question. Patrons probably read this as closely, and like it as much, as the user agreements on software. Conversely, some libraries place their use policies behind a log-in, which means that users don't know the policies until they log in, which seems paradoxical.[2]

The FAQ or "About This Service" page is an approachable way to communicate service policy. The title is less unfriendly, and the policy statement is framed as something a user may wish to know more about, rather than as limitations framed by the library. Such web pages may also contain information about the service, such as how long it has been operational, statistics on number of questions received, profiles of librarians, and so forth. Sometimes the FAQ is combined with the policies, as in the example in figure 5-1, if both are short.

Wording the Policy

As with the examples in figure 5-1, policies can be short. Brevity is a virtue; if you are not good at it, have someone else read your policy draft with a red pen. If you feel the need to include many details in your policy, consider a brief and a long version, or break the policy into sections with anchors so that people can get to the part they want quickly.

Policies are easily found by looking at other library websites and noting those features you like best. Some libraries adopt a conversational tone ("We'll answer questions about a range of topics . . .") and provide examples of the kinds of questions that can be asked ("How many people live in Beijing?" "What foods were eaten by the Aztecs?"). Determine first what you want to communicate and then how to present it in the most clear and appropriate way for your audience.

Where you can, use positive words. Say what the service will do, not what it will not do. Some negative language may be needed, as when you are addressing prohibition of abuse and blocking patrons, but reserve it for where it is needed. Avoid having your policy read like a list of pool rules.

Scope and Enforcement

At my library, less than 3 percent of our virtual reference questions are from unaffiliated users with questions that fall outside the scope of our service. At one time (during 2002), our virtual reference service came up consistently as the third result in Google searches for "ask a librarian," and we still had very few questions that did not meet the parameters of our service. In truth, few people are likely to just stumble across a library's virtual reference service. Most libraries probably have more unaffiliated walk-in patrons than virtual patrons. Nonetheless, it is a good idea to have a policy in place to guide both patrons and staff.

Many libraries enforce service policies only loosely. It is in our nature as reference librarians to be helpful and to at least direct the patron to a more appropriate place to ask their question. Sometimes it takes only a few minutes to be extremely helpful. For example, a student from a university in England once contacted my library's Ask a Librarian service. He was writing a paper on a specific classical musician and needed assistance finding scholarly articles. This was out of the scope of our service since it was not specific to our library, and I could not provide him with access to my library's subscription article databases. Nevertheless, in about two minutes I found that his university library had a subscription to one of the major music databases as well as an e-mail reference service. I was able to direct him to an appropriate resource and a place to ask follow-up questions, for which I received profuse thanks. Sometimes patrons are floundering in a sea of information and it is not difficult to throw them a rope.

FIGURE 5-1 EXAMPLE VIRTUAL REFERENCE POLICY AND FAQ

Information About AskAmes

WHO STAFFS THIS SERVICE?

Our service is staffed by librarians. We work from the Information Desk on the 1st floor of the Ames Library where we also provide assistance in person and over the phone. Since we help a lot of patrons, there may, on occasion, be slight delays in responding to your chat or IM request, but we make every effort to provide fast service to all patrons.

WHAT ARE THE HOURS OF OPERATION?

AskAmes is available during regular <u>Information Desk hours</u>.

HOW DOES ASKAMES WORK?

You can contact us any time you have a research or library-related question online via chat. You can also contact us using your home or cell phone, by e-mail, or just by coming to the Information Desk using the information provided in the lower left-hand column.

WHO CAN USE ASKAMES?

Chat assistance is primarily intended as service for the IWU Community. If you are not a current affiliate, we're happy to refer you to a service that might be more appropriate.

DO YOU SAVE THE TRANSCRIPTS?

Transcripts may be reviewed for evaluation and research purposes. All personal information will be removed and destroyed.

WHAT IS IM AND HOW DOES IT WORK?

IM stands for "Instant Message," and refers to software like AOL Instant Messenger (AIM) which can be used to have a live conversation with a librarian. To contact us, send a message from your IM software to our Screen Name, AskAmes.

WHICH IM NETWORK DO YOU USE?

We have accounts on AOL Instant Messenger (AIM), Google Talk, Yahoo! Messenger and MSN Messenger, all with the same Screen Name, AskAmes. Add us to your Buddy List now!

NO IM SOFTWARE?

If you do not wish to download and install instant messaging software on your computer, we encourage you to send us a message using the widget embedded on the left side of the library web pages.

WHAT IS A WIDGET?

The AskAmes widget allows people who are using the Ames Library website to ask a librarian any questions they might have along the way. No registration is required. To start chatting, type your question in the lower box that says, "Type Here," and hit enter to send your message.

When defining what is out of scope for your service, it is a good idea to keep in-person services policies in mind to promote consistency or at least logic. In-person use of article databases (with librarian assistance) may be possible and supported by your library, but remote use of article databases may be restricted by license to cardholders at your library, making it impossible for your virtual reference service to assist unaffiliated users with article searches. This results in understandably inconsistent in-person and virtual service policies. If your library does not have service policies for in-person and telephone reference, this is a good time to set such policies, perhaps making one cohesive policy for all of your reference service.

Privacy

Privacy is a big issue for libraries. Librarians have defied authorities and even gone to jail to protect the privacy of patron records. It is something that many librarians feel passionate about as individuals, and it is a part of the ALA Code of Ethics. In virtual reference, privacy of the individual has new threats for both the patron and the librarian. What data are saved, for how long, how they will be used, and who can see them are all questions that should be addressed in both patron policies and internal staff policies. Virtual reference transactions should be taken into consideration, along with patron circulation records, when your library formulates its policies regarding USA Patriot Act requests and other requests for information from law enforcement.

Patrons

It is likely that patrons will not read your privacy policy, even though we know they should. As a library, you still must have a policy, and you should post it visibly. Build a link to it in the place most likely for anyone who cares to read it to be able to find it, such as on the home page of your virtual reference service. There is nothing wrong, of course, with placing the text of the policy right on the virtual reference home page, but be cognizant of elements of good design.

STORED DATA, CHAT

In almost all virtual reference services, transcripts are stored. Patron data may or may not be stored, and elimination of patron identifying data is one of the features of commercial virtual reference packages. It is common for some data to be present—for example, data gathered through a web form when the patron entered the service—but nothing that links the data about a patron to his specific transcript.

STORED DATA, IM

Instant messaging does not have the administrative features of the commercial virtual reference products. There is no option to decouple the patron's IM screen name from the transcript. When libraries are storing transcripts, this is an important factor, even though most patrons do not use their real names as their screen names.

Transcripts are also stored on the servers of the IM service: AOL has transcripts of all AIM transcripts, Google has the gTalk transcripts, and so forth. This is something patrons may or may not be aware of. Ostensibly, they have read the user agreement when they signed up for their IM account and know this. In reality, these agreements are long and probably not read in depth by most people. The library has no control over what gets stored on the servers of IM providers. Notably, Meebo does allow users to opt out of having their Meebo IMs stored on the Meebo servers. Google Talk also allows users to set a chat as "off the record," in which case the transcript is not stored.

Considering the things people talk about using IM—dates they've been on, parties—the questions they ask of the library may be the least of their concerns as far as privacy. A 2000 Pew report revealed that young adults (age 18–26) were far less concerned with online privacy than older adults (50–64), and that 54 percent of online users had provided personal information as a prerequisite for using a website.[3] As for online communications, 19 percent of American teens choose IM as the way to communicate when they want a conversation to be private—the telephone is still the top choice for private conversations.[4]

People who are really trying to keep their conversations private and anonymous can do so by taking precautions on their end. They can use fake information when setting up their IM accounts or mask their computer's IP address, among other tricks. In short, if a person is engaging in conversations they want kept secret or fear will cause them to be investigated, they can take protective measures.

Libraries cannot control the storage of transcripts completely, but how a library handles its IM transcripts is an important consideration: how long they are stored, whether they go through measures to remove patron screen names, who sees the transcripts. This information should be part of the publicly viewable patron privacy policy. Despite the lack of library control over this information, IM is still a service worth offering. It is one of a suite of ways by which patrons can ask libraries questions, and if a patron feels that a question is safer being asked another way, the telephone and in-person contact are available options.

E-MAIL

Since it is necessary to have a patron's e-mail address to send a reply, this is not a particularly private mode of communication. E-mail addresses are generally stored with the accompanying questions to allow for follow-up. Again, users can take precautions to set up an untraceable account to ensure their own privacy. Libraries do need to take measures on their end as far as how long the transcripts are kept and who can view them. Again, this policy information should be available to patrons.

ASKING FOR ID TO ENTER THE SERVICE

Some libraries require patrons to authenticate as part of their affiliated user group before asking questions of their virtual reference service. It is then the library's responsibility to ensure that the authentication data are not linked to a particular transaction. Talk with your virtual reference software vendor or local IT department (if they have set up the authentication mechanism) to verify what is being done to protect patron privacy.

HOW LONG TRANSCRIPTS ARE STORED

Retaining transcripts is easy with computer storage so inexpensive. Since space is not a consideration, libraries need to look at other factors in deciding how long to store transcripts. What will the transcripts be used for? Is there a length of time after which they are out of date (necessary to think about if you are using them for training)? Does length of storage affect the security of the transcripts and increase the library's liability? If you have been able to take care of this last question through technical means, then it is not an issue. And remember that the transcripts may exist elsewhere. Nonetheless, determine how long transcripts for e-mail, chat, IM, and other modes are to be retained and stick to that schedule. Include your retention policy in your privacy policy. Fundamentally, ask how long your library really needs to have every transcript.

WHO SEES THE TRANSCRIPTS

With all modes of online communication, where transcripts are stored for any length of time it is vital to control who can view them and why. It is common to allow all staff who provide virtual reference service to view all transcripts. Some software allows more refinement whereby librarians can view their transcripts but not the transcripts of other librarians. The administrator of the service almost always has access to all transcripts. In consortial arrangements, librarians outside the local library may have access to transcripts. Who can see transcripts is a factor for both patron privacy and staff comfort. Librarians or others who are not part of the virtual reference service should not have access to transcripts, particularly if they include patron data. If you use transcripts for a research study that includes researchers from outside your institution, acceptable practice demands that any identifying information about patrons or individual librarians be removed.

WHAT THE TRANSCRIPTS ARE USED FOR

Patrons probably would like to know, if they are reading your policies, why you are saving the transcripts. What will you be using them for, anyway? Quality review is a common reason and one patrons may appreciate. Training is another reason and one tied to quality as well. Research and assessment, current or in the future, are other reasons transcripts are saved. Whatever the case, do explain it in your policy and reiterate that patron identifying information is removed.

A LAST NOTE ON PATRON PRIVACY

To be practical, our policies tell patrons only what we are doing to protect them and what liabilities they take on by using the service. Libraries sometimes lose their battles to protect patron privacy. It is best, therefore, to have in place as much technical infrastructure for clearing away patron data or breaking all links between personal patron information and the questions they ask. When push comes to subpoena, the real way to protect privacy is to have no information to give.

Staff

Do staff have an expectation of privacy of their work communications? That would be another book. But as it pertains to virtual reference, opinions are divided about transcript review. Supervisors like it for the opportunities it gives for training and quality assessment. Some librarians and staff are less comfortable with it because being reviewed in this way is new and may feel threatening. There is more discussion of transcript review in other chapters of this book. It should be clear in your internal policies if transcripts will be reviewed and by whom. If you allow all virtual reference staff to view all transcripts, then it should be clear what counts as acceptable conduct and what a librarian who sees a problem in a transcript should do. Collegiality in this area may be new, especially if the library's desk has been single-staffed, so provide guidelines, or at least guidance, to avoid ruffled feathers.

The privacy of the librarian vis-à-vis the patron is another issue. Some libraries maintain a virtual reference presence that presents all staff under the same name, such as "librarian at ZYX Library." This does preserve a layer of privacy for the librarian and presents a single service. Some libraries prefer that librarians appear more personal, so they encourage or require use of individualized screen names such as "Betsy at ZYX Library." This decision should be made in light of your other policies. Do staff wear name tags? Are individual phone numbers advertised? Are you promoting a liaison role with academic departments or leaving your staff open to stalking? Your type and size of library may influence these decisions. Know that, depending on their past experiences, staff may be more or less comfortable with using their names in such a public way. Consider first names only or initials as a way to maintain some privacy while still maintaining approachability and the option for patrons to make a second contact with a librarian with whom they have already worked.

Copyright Issues

Librarians cannot help but be aware that the digital environment raises a lot of copyright issues. Virtual reference is part of that environment, so the issues carry over. Here, I would advise being conservative in what your library provides in terms of digital copies of print or online documents. Do not circumvent your interlibrary loan department by sending materials to other libraries or nonaffiliated users. You may be violating copyright or the licensing agreements for your electronic subscriptions. It is just not worth the risk.

Providing material for affiliated patrons is more of a gray area. I am not a lawyer, so I cannot say if it is legal to provide one of your patrons with a copy of an article from an online database or a scanned copy from a print journal. This practice should follow what you would do for a telephone patron. If you don't have a policy for that, write one, and perhaps consult your legal counsel.

At my library, we do not provide electronic copies of articles (or other material) on demand for our patrons. We do not want the virtual reference service to become a document delivery service. For online articles, we show patrons how to obtain the articles themselves. We have a document delivery service (fee-based) for patrons who do not wish to come into the library for print materials. The exception to this policy is when there is a technical problem with a patron accessing an electronic subscription. If we are able to access the material, then we send the material needed. As of yet, we know of no patrons abusing this service by claiming access problems.

Copying, or not, of materials can be an internal policy. If you receive many requests for this service and it is not something you provide through virtual reference, then you might want to make it part of your public policy so that you can refer to the stated policy.

Obscenities, Nuisances, and Other Bad Behavior

I hear many librarians new to virtual reference voice concern over how patrons will behave online. Does the anonymous nature of the interaction lead to abuses of the service? Perhaps. But probably less often than might be predicted. Research by the AskColorado collaborative found that interactions in which patrons were abusive or rude were rare, but policies did need to be in place to guide librarians in the proper response.[5] Some software (including all IM) allows a user to be blocked. A warning about why the particular behavior is inappropriate and that blocking will follow is good practice. There are also times when it is appropriate to just "hang up." The telephone is a great analogy here. How do you handle a patron who is swearing at you? It all depends on circumstances; there are times when you try to calm the patron down, and times when you end the conversation.

Sometimes the questions being asked are outside the stated scope of the service yet the patron persists. I am not here talking about obscene "questions" but about patrons demanding answers you cannot provide, access to your subscription databases, or other assistance outside your policy. Scope is, of course, part of your policy, but the library should provide guidance for staff on what to do if a patron pushes on that policy.

Here again, policies about expected behavior and the consequences should mirror the policies that exist for in-person and telephone patrons. Post this as part of your virtual reference policies or general patron conduct policies.

Exercise 5-2 is a follow-up to the more casual small-group conversation on service philosophies (exercise 5-1). It is a group discussion on policy areas for virtual reference and the appropriate policies for your library. Several options for structuring this exercise are presented, so you may decide that a free-form discussion fits your library's style or that starting from a draft policy or a look at other libraries' policies (figure 5-1) is the more productive way to initiate the discussion.

NOTES

1. Joseph Fennewald, "Same Questions, Different Venue: An Analysis of In-person and Online Questions," *Reference Librarian* 46, nos. 95/96 (2006): 21–35.
2. M. Kathleen Kern and Esther Gillie, "Virtual Reference Policies: An Examination of Current Practice in Various Organizations," in *The Virtual Reference Experience: Integrating Theory into Practice*, ed. R. David Lankes et al., 165–184 (New York: Neal-Schuman, 2004); also presented at the Virtual Desk Reference Conference, San Antonio, TX, November 2003, http://data.webjunction.org/wj/documents/12686.pdf.
3. Susannah Fox et al., "Trust and Privacy Online: Why Americans Want to Rewrite the Rules," Report from the Pew Internet and American Life Project, August 20, 2000, www.pewinternet.org/pdfs/PIP_Trust_Privacy_Report.pdf.
4. Amanda Lenhart and Mary Madden, "Teens, Privacy, and Online Social Networks: How Teens Manage Their Online Identities and Personal Information in the Age of MySpace," Report from the Pew Internet and American Life Project, April 18, 2007, www.pewinternet.org/pdfs/PIP_Teens_Privacy_SNS_Report_Final.pdf.
5. In a study conducted by the AskColorado consortium, "1369 transactions were categorized and analyzed, 497 from 2003 and 872 from 2004. Of these, eighty-nine (6.50%) were found to be inappropriate in some manner. Thirty-five were categorized 'goofing around' (2.56%), forty-two were 'rude' (3.07%), and a total of twelve transactions were categorized as 'offensive' (0.88%). Results from 2003 and 2004 were different. Of the 497 transactions analyzed for 2003, a total of forty-three were inappropriate in some manner (8.65%). For 2004, forty-six of 972 were inappropriate (4.73%)." Sarah Naper and Jack Maness, "Assessing Inappropriate Use of AskColorado," AskColorado Collaborative Virtual Reference Quality Assurance and Evaluation Committee, November 10, 2005, www.aclin.org/reference/committees/qa/inappropriate_use.pdf.

Service Policies: Setting Our Expectations

This is an area where discussion is better than brainstorming. The purpose is to get a measure of staff feelings around important areas of service and policy. There are several ways to start this discussion:

1. Present possible policies (verbally, so that the focus is on the policy content, not on wordsmithing); or
2. Present policies from other libraries, showing their different approaches to their service; or
3. Start with a detailed examination of your current library policies. Focus on how to make virtual policies comply, or on whether current policies should be revised.

In any case, your library's current policies should be examined side by side with your virtual reference policies, but this may not be where you want to start.

I have found that the most fruitful areas for policy discussion are

- ➤ Priority of service
- ➤ Unaffiliated patrons/out-of-scope questions
- ➤ Time limitations for chat and time-to-response for e-mail
- ➤ Types of questions that will be answered
- ➤ Response to harassing users

CHAPTER 6

Selecting Software

You can't offer a virtual reference service without using some type of software. Software must be in place before training can start, and software may affect the type of service you offer, how you staff, and what data you can collect. Software involves some important decisions, but it should not be where you start.

It might be surprising to find a chapter on software selection so late in a book about virtual reference, but this reflects my philosophy about where in the decision-making process software should be. Software changes. It even goes away. Tomorrow there will be something new. Good sense says to base your software choices around a sound idea of what you want the service to offer your patrons, combined with how it will work for the library staff.

Entire books have been written about selecting virtual reference software. I offer a more streamlined approach. The matrix in worksheet 6-1 helps you keep track of software features and library priorities. This chapter explains some of the choices available and how they can affect your service. Keep in mind that software changes constantly; I focus on aspects that are more likely to remain constant.

The Basics: Text-Based Communication

Online communication breaks into two basic divisions: those that happen in real time (synchronous), and those in which significant time elapses between sending and receipt of communication (asynchronous). This is like the difference between a telephone call and a posted letter. There is an imperceptible delay while the voice communication is transmitted, but it is a conversation. With the posted letter, the sending and response are delayed; we may be able to discuss a topic by letter, but many of the elements of a back-and-forth conversation are missing. This difference in time to communicate is a factor in deciding if information is best conveyed by telephone or mail.

FEATURE	IMPORTANCE 0 = DO NOT WANT 1 = NOT REALLY NEEDED 4 = MUST HAVE	SOFTWARE 1	SOFTWARE 2	SOFTWARE 3
System and software requirements				
Compatible with most browsers/operating systems				
Does not require software download				
Low bandwidth requirements				
Local hosting of software				
Vendor hosting of software				
Look and feel				
Customizable look/ability to brand				
Question entry form				
User does not need to have an account				
Ease of use/familiarity				
Supports user authentication				
Communication				
Co-browsing				
Send/share files				
Canned messages				
"Push" pages without co-browsing				
E-mail integration				
Voice-over-IP				
Video-chat				
Collaborative				
Transfer between operators				
Operator-to-operator chat				
Shared queue				
Backup or after-hours service				

(cont.)

FEATURE	IMPORTANCE 0 = DO NOT WANT 1 = NOT REALLY NEEDED 4 = MUST HAVE	SOFTWARE 1	SOFTWARE 2	SOFTWARE 3
Administrative				
Transcripts saved				
Statistical reports				
Ability to set access levels				
Marketability (name recognition)				
Cost				
Comments				
Ranking				

Rank software needs on a 0–4 scale. 0 means that this is a feature you *do not want*. 4 means that a feature is *required*; without it you will not consider the software. 1–3 are increasing degrees of desirability. It is suggested that this be one of the last exercises, since software should not drive your other decisions, with the exception of training.

Next, evaluate the software under consideration in terms of how it meets the requirements. +, ✓, – is an easy system to use. + means the software does this well, – is a missing feature or one that does not work well, ✓ means the feature is present but does not stand out or you are unable to judge the quality. (✓ will likely be used only infrequently.)

The Asynchronous: E-mail and Text Messaging

E-MAIL

E-mail is the oldest form of virtual reference in libraries. It is pervasive in many people's work and private lives. For those who are online regularly it has, in some measure, taken the place of memos, mailed letters, and even telephone calls. E-mail has the advantage of being able to be stored and referred to later. It is an important communication tool and one libraries should seriously consider if they do not already provide this service.

E-mail systems are plentiful. Most librarians have e-mail accounts as part of their job and are expected to use it for interorganizational communications. Patrons in the library can use e-mail through free web browser–based services even if they do not have access to the Internet at home or work. Since e-mail systems allow messages to be sent from one e-mail system to another, libraries may choose to use their existing e-mail software and servers to answer e-mail reference questions.

Some libraries use e-mail software that is different from that used for their work communications, for a variety of reasons:

➤ Integration with chat software, which allows for chats to be moved to e-mail easily
➤ Separation of reference e-mail from personal e-mail
➤ Sharing one account that all e-mail comes into (for security, some organizations do not allow account sharing on their regular e-mail system)
➤ Ability to advertise a single e-mail address for e-mail reference with routing to individual librarians for reply while keeping the e-mail within a shared platform
➤ Administration of e-mail service: monitoring of routing, time-to-answer reports, tracking of question status (e.g., read, completed, unanswered, in-process), transcript review, statistics
➤ Collaborative features, such as routing, for consortia

TEXT MESSAGING

Text messaging is not now widely adopted by libraries. But it is a text-based form of communication and, from a technological standpoint, one that is a proven and stable platform for communication. The real question here is whether text messaging is something our patrons will use for asking questions. The current limitation of 160 characters may limit not only the librarian but the patron. Asking for help finding articles for a paper is different from arranging a time to meet your best friend for coffee, and this is a distinction patrons are likely to make. On the other hand, simple requests for a call number or library hours could be handled via text messaging, and some libraries have set up scripts, or "bots," to handle these simple questions.

Since text messaging is not a technology with a strong presence in libraries, I include more detail in chapter 14, on emerging technologies.

The Synchronous

Synchronous communication is what is most often thought of (at least in 2008) when librarians read the words *virtual reference.* It is the involvement of libraries in providing service to patrons through chat that really launched the term *virtual reference* and precipitated its adoption in a large number of libraries worldwide.

Totally apart from any particular software platform, what you want from this feature is the ability to type and send text to a patron and have it received within seconds (or less) and for the patron to type and send text back to you. This is what creates the appealing conversational aspect of chat virtual reference.

CHAT VS. IM FOR TEXT COMMUNICATION

As far as the type-text-and-send-it aspects of the software, there is little difference in function between chat and IM software. On the patron side, IM often has a more streamlined, or "cleaner," look than chat, particularly if other features are presented such as co-browsing. On the librarian side, the screen for chat is less streamlined, since it must include the options of canned messages, forwarding, and the like.

The major differences between chat and IM, from the user perspective, are how patrons reach the library, familiarity of the interface, and what steps are necessary before they talk to the librarian (see below).

Embedded IM is a sort of IM/chat hybrid. It provides an HTML code to include a text box that is then embedded in the library's web page. (Individuals can do this too. It is not a library-specific application.) Patrons can type into the box, and the library receives the text in an interface that probably looks a lot like an IM interface. The simplicity for the patron is that no account is required. There is no form to fill out; it is just a simple box. It does lack the advanced features of commercial IM software. See the Library Field Report "MeeboMe at Samford University" for more details on this software.

AFTER-HOURS SERVICE

Some library software vendors have contract employees who provide service to patrons during hours when the library is not open. There is a fairly substantial cost involved, but your library may find the availability of live 24/7 service to be worth it. Libraries in consortia also extend their hours of chat assistance, sometimes to 24/7 hours, by partnering with libraries that offer service at different hours—often libraries in other countries or time zones.

After-hours service may also be provided through e-mail, although that is not really 24/7 service. If your pharmacy advertised 24/7 service but after 5:00 p.m. you could only leave a message for the prescription to be filled the next day, you would hardly view this as service around the clock.

Full-Featured Communication

There can be more to virtual reference than sending and receiving text. The more "advanced" features of virtual reference software have many advocates and also detractors. In the interest of full disclosure, I admit my current bias toward simple communication and using what the patron uses. I also appreciate some of the features of commercial software, such as the data collection and collaborative possibilities. I guess you could say that I want simplicity for the patron and complexity for the librarian/service administrator. Whatever my biases, your library must choose software based

Meebo Me at Samford University, an Interview with an Early Adopter

When did Samford begin using Meebo?

We began using Meebo in January 2007.

Why did you decide to adopt the service?

We had been using Trillian as a chat aggregator for three chat accounts. Upgrades to the MSN chat client resulted in frequent loss of connection with Trillian. When multiple attempts to resolve this issue failed, I decided to try using GAIM, which I knew of from our first search for aggregators. GAIM also seemed to experience connection problems with MSN. Meebo was new to me; I found it by doing some searching on library sites and decided to give it a try. We were pleased, even though Meebo had some limitations; the MeeboMe chat widget available for use on our website really sold us on Meebo, though. We haven't looked back.

Did Meebo replace any preexisting virtual reference services? If so, which ones and why?

It replaced Trillian, as I mentioned above, and resulted in our adding two more chat accounts to our repertoire, Google Talk and ICQ.

What do you view as Meebo's strong points?

The chat box and its web platform.

Its weaknesses?

Sending live links to users doesn't work with the MeeboMe widget. I would also like a color change to occur to tabs in IE7 [Internet Explorer] when Meebo receives a message. As it is, the text flashes, and there is a soft sound; color would help to get my attention when I already have several tabs beyond Meebo open.

How have virtual reference statistics changed since you began using Meebo?

We've seen our numbers of chat transactions double, but since we started using Meebo and MeeboMe at the same time, I don't know which might be of greater influence. I do assume, from some comments I've heard, that the MeeboMe widget has made the difference.

How have patrons reacted to the service?

We've heard very positive comments related to the MeeboMe widget.

Lori Northrup, Reference Department Coordinator,
Samford University, Birmingham, Alabama

Interview by Lena Singer

on your patrons' needs and the needs of your organization. Software is continually being developed, and next year today's detractors could be praising the more full-featured virtual reference software.

Co-browsing, Page Pushing, and Other Sharing (Reach-out Software)

One of the factors that really launched the virtual reference movement was the capability to share a web browser with the patron. In 2003, this was all the rage, and every library that wanted virtual reference wanted to co-browse. Co-browsing is a two-way situation in which the librarian and the patron can both control the navigation of web pages and online databases. Anything the librarian does in the co-browse window is seen by the patron, and anything done by the patron is seen by the librarian. This has obvious implications for instruction, and it is easy to see why librarians are interested in this feature.

What was not predicted is the extent to which patrons would not seem to care about co-browsing and the difficulties software vendors would have designing co-browse to be compatible with the myriad database platforms, patron authentication protocols, browsers, and operating systems. Patrons remarked more on the online availability of the librarian than on the coolness of the co-browse. (This should really make librarians feel good about the value users place on us.) Furthermore, the unreliability of co-browsing led some libraries to ignore this feature of their virtual reference software and to instead instruct patrons through text communication. When co-browsing improved but was still less than perfect, these libraries did not return to using this feature. I feel for the vendors; librarians really pushed development of co-browse for years, and now most libraries place greater priority on other features.

Page pushing allows the librarian to send a static web page, which is basically an online screen shot. Pages can be pushed in succession to create a sort of slideshow of a step-by-step process. For the user to follow along, she re-creates the steps in another browser window. URLs can also be sent to a patron through virtual reference software, and the pages launch in another window.

File sharing is another sharing feature, and libraries have used this to send tutorials and instructions to patrons. Rarely is file sharing used to send articles or copyrighted content, for rather obvious reasons.

The last of the reaching-out features is one not present in library software, but one employed by contact center software used on retail and help desk websites. This feature allows the librarian to initiate a conversation with a patron who is using the library's website but has made no attempt to ask a question. The librarian is alerted to a patron who has been on a web page for a while and has the option of asking him if he would like assistance. Libraries generally view this retail approach as intrusive, and I have been unable to find libraries that use this feature.

VoIP

Several libraries have forayed into live video or online voice communications. I address video in chapter 14, since it does not have widespread use in libraries, commercial call centers, or the general population (excluding "adult" webcams). I include voice-over-Internet protocol (VoIP) in this chapter because it is a feature of contact center software and is present with IM. It is also under consideration for development by library vendors, but this depends on the demand from libraries.

Simply put, VoIP allows people to use the Internet like a telephone, transmitting and receiving audio in real time. A microphone and speakers or a headset are essential pieces of hardware for sending and receiving audio over the computer. Some virtual reference and call center software has live audio, which allows for transfer of a patron from the text environment to voice. It also combines several modes of communication into one contact point, and the software may allow for the archiving of voice communications.

Patrons may also use VoIP to initiate communication with a library through the telephone, since VoIP allows this functionality. You are unlikely to know that a patron is calling you using her own VoIP account unless you are told so. Thus, libraries can serve users with VoIP technology without using VoIP themselves. Internet providers are starting to offer this as a for-fee service and marketing it as a way to replace landline telephone service at home.

There are also free VoIP services such as Skype, which started up in 2003. Skype has 75 million registered users, and an estimated 6 million have been online at one time.[1] The free services require that both the caller and the callee use the same free network. Skype and other services are seen by many IT departments as security or privacy risks and are banned for use over their networks. This is certainly a consideration for any library thinking about offering reference using a free VoIP network. It is prudent to find out your institution's policy before embarking on a service that will be shut down because it violates university or local government policy.

I wonder how many patrons would make use of an Internet-based audio service rather than just calling on their cell phones. The Library Field Report "VoIP Wouldn't Work for Me" details the myriad difficulties encountered in using VoIP to enhance IM encounters. On the other hand, your library may like to be a pioneer, or you may be aware that your population has a high demand for voice communication. Perhaps, by the time you are reading this, VoIP has been integrated into commercial virtual reference products.

Requirements for Hardware and Software

Compatibility

We've come to expect broad compatibility between software and operating systems. We can open MS Office documents on a Mac now, after all. We expect the same compatibility between websites and the most popular web browsers. Virtual reference software is not the place to lower your standards.

Apart from the known co-browsing problems, you should confirm compatibility for the other parts of the software (text communication, VoIP, librarian interface) with the most popular operating systems and browsers used by your community. This does vary by community. Your IT department may be able to provide this information, since it is sometimes collected as part of website use logs.

If there are specific plug-ins needed or browser configurations, be sure that these are installed/configured on your library's computers. For example, some virtual reference software does not work properly if pop-up blockers are in use. This can be an issue on the librarian side as well.

Voice-over-IP
Wouldn't Work for Me

We started a chat reference pilot at my library a couple of years ago and decided to use instant messaging. Dedicated virtual reference programs have more features, but we wanted something cheap and easy to use. We went with Trillian, which is one of several multiprotocol IM applications.

We used the free Trillian Basic and got along fine, but I was curious about what features of Trillian Pro we might use. Voice-over-IP seemed a logical feature to test.

I first thought of using VoIP for chat reference when my college-age nephew visited for a couple of weeks. At night he spent much of his time playing the multiplayer online game *World of Warcraft* and chatting through his headset with friends around the country. Perhaps, I thought, games like this would be popular enough with college students that a large number of them would have the headsets necessary to make VoIP reference work. Even if they didn't have a headset, I could always talk to them and save myself some typing.

I got a headset and started playing around with it, using Google Talk with a colleague of mine across the country. I found it very easy to use. Then I upgraded to Trillian Pro and got ready for business.

That's when the project stalled. I had the headset. I had Trillian Pro, which supposedly supported VoIP. I knew that at least two of the IM clients I was using through Trillian supported VoIP—Google Talk and AOL Instant Messenger (AIM). But I couldn't get either to work. I especially wanted AIM to work, because that is by far the most popular IM client our students use to contact the library, but no luck.

We would try to make calls, and the calls would just hang there, with the initiator of the call waiting and the recipient never receiving any notice of the incoming call. I did some poking around on the Web and found I was not alone, that other people had experienced similar problems. I had played around with several other multiprotocol IM applications and none seemed to offer this feature or make it work. This feature would work consistently only if we restricted ourselves to one IM client or invested more time and money into the project, which no one wanted to do.

In the end, there were just too many barriers: the librarian needed a headset, the student needed at least speakers, the student had to come in via an IM client that supported VoIP, the librarian had to be aware of that and initiate the VoIP call, and the intervening software needed to actually work. I just couldn't overcome all the obstacles, so I had to abandon the project. Good thing I'm a fast typist.

Wayne Bivens-Tatum, Philosophy and Religion Librarian,
Princeton University Library

When choosing software remember: you can require your staff to use specific browsers and configurations, but you have no control over your patron's software (or hardware) choices.

Barriers to Use: Downloads and Accounts

If the patron needs to download any software, chances are they will not use your service. Many are just following good Internet security practices by not downloading unknown software. Mostly, though, they can't be bothered to take this step.

Some services, such as IM, require that the patron have an account. This is not a barrier for patrons who already have signed up for accounts for other reasons. It is a barrier for patrons who are not already using IM (or whatever service) because, being realistic, no patron is going to sign up for an account just to ask the library a question.

Requirements for Your Library

As already mentioned, you (or your IT staff) can control the configurations for operating systems and browsers for your staff computers. There are still some considerations when it comes to the software and hardware requirements of virtual reference systems.

Who hosts the software? Does the library need to provide server space and maintenance? This may not be a big deal with your IT staff. Then again, it may be. Find this out early, for it will have a budgetary impact as well.

Is the software being used compatible with IT policies? Usually if there is a conflict between IT policies and the software the library is considering, it is around security issues. Read about the possible security issues and then talk to your IT department again. Seek a solution that meets their requirements and still allows the library to offer the service that it wants to provide.

Accessibility

Can patrons who use screen readers or other assistive devices still make use of your virtual reference software? In the best of cases, your prospective software vendor can answer this question. For free services this information may be provided in the online documentation. If no documentation is available, try searching online for user commentary. Testing the software is always an option, but if you are unfamiliar with screen readers and assistive software, consult someone who has expertise in this area. If compatibility is indeterminable, the basic question is whether you are providing an equivalent service to users with disabilities. Is offering reference service through other channels such as telephone or e-mail considered an equitable accommodation? Of course, this is a legal question, so your library can consult legal counsel. It is, however, unlikely that this is the first time your library had to examine its services and software for accessibility, and there are generally resources available. Your city government or campus administration may have a department that helps with this and other ADA compliance questions.

Sometimes the Best Choice Is Both

Your library may not find all the features it wants in one software package. This can result in choosing the closest match, or it may mean that you choose side-by-side services with two different types of software. This is happening in some libraries now with IM and chat software, two applications that reach different user groups.[2] Melissa Records at the Champaign (Illinois) Public Library states their philosophy behind offering multiple virtual reference channels:

> It's all about convenience. We chose to use IM reference because it is convenient for many customers. It is the preferred form of communication for a large number of people and it requires no extra software or learning curve. We chose AskAway [using QuestionPoint software] so that we could provide our customers with the convenience of 24/7 reference services.[3]

Things Only the Librarians Care About

Some features may be very important to your library and your staff but have little impact on the service provided during a specific transaction and no visibility to your patrons. They may or may not improve service overall. Some libraries find the following features essential; others see them as "nice to have." Determining their importance is a factor in deciding between commercial chat software and free services like IM and some shareware applications.

Canned Messages and Other Time Savers

Canned messages allow the librarian to select from a pre-scripted list of messages that can be quickly sent to a patron. The text appears in the librarian's text box and can then be sent. This is useful for frequently used messages, such as "please hold for two minutes while I search for this information," and for sending links to commonly used web pages. Sometimes canned messages can be set up to send lists of instructions, but this can lead to a lot of text appearing on the patron's screen all at once. Instead the library might want to link to a web page with instructions, or just step the patron through the process.

Auto-response messages can be set up in some systems to greet patrons automatically when they are picked up out of a queue. This makes the first message to patrons appear almost instantly as soon as they are claimed by a librarian. Auto-response messages may also appear without librarian involvement if a patron has been waiting in queue without his question being claimed—such as to reassure the patron that a librarian will be with him soon. Software varies, but the administrator may be able to set the wording of this message, how long the patron has to wait to receive this message, and if the message appears when librarians are helping other patrons. A third type of auto-response message is sent after the close of an interaction. These might ask the user to take a survey or provide instructions on how to save his transcript.

These canned and auto-response messages save time and relieve some pressure to type quickly, but they can sound robotic and pre-scripted, which of course they are. Some systems allow for individualized messages specific to a librarian, which allows for a more personal voice to be present in canned messages. Instant messaging does not include canned message and auto-reply capabilities, but it is common for libraries to create web pages with canned text that can be copied and pasted into the text box.

Administrative and Assessment Tools

MANAGEMENT

Tools for the administrator add elements of control and customization to the management of virtual reference. They allow designation of groups of employees with different rights in terms of viewing transcripts, creating individual librarian accounts, and monitoring workflow issues such as time-to-response and number of questions answered. Creation of queues for different types of patrons, subjects, and libraries is possible. This feature can be used in consortia, but also in larger libraries and in library systems with multiple branches. These features are present in different commercial chat software packages but are largely absent from IM.

CUSTOMIZATION

Local customization of the look of the virtual reference environment may be possible. Branding is important to most libraries, so the ability to replace the vendor's brand with the library logo or service name is a nice feature, though probably not one that will seriously affect a decision to purchase. Changing form elements on the screen where the patron enters the service is more central to how users approach the virtual reference environment for both chat and e-mail interactions. Patrons may be turned away by lengthy forms for several reasons. They may not wish to invest the time for what they see as a simple question. They may find the form intrusive. Worst of all, they may read a form that is required to start a chat as an e-mail web form and not as the entry for a live interaction. In these cases the patron may leave without ever asking a question, or may send a question formatted as she would for an e-mail and immediately leave the page. With the latter, the library will have a way to respond to the patron, if she has left an e-mail address. With the former, the patron never leaves a question and believes that the library does not have a chat reference service.

Here are a few questions to ask as you evaluate the customization aspects of virtual reference software:

- ➤ Can you change the order of elements in the form?
- ➤ Can you control which elements are required and which are optional?
- ➤ Can you choose the form elements, or are they preset by the vendor?
- ➤ Can the user select an "anonymous" option rather than providing a name or e-mail address?
- ➤ How much can you change the overall look, colors, or branding of the interface?
- ➤ How important to you are the different types of customization?

ASSESSMENT

Assessment is an important part of a successful service (see chapter 13 for a deeper discussion of this topic). Assessment can be done (and quite well) without built-in assessment tools, but these tools do make the collection and processing of data easier. As of yet, no tool will tell you what the data actually mean for the library—this is dependent on local factors.

Types of information that may be stored are

- ➤ Transcripts
- ➤ Metadata about the questions: time and date received, time and date completed, librarians who handled the question, length of chat/IM interaction

➤ Time spent waiting in queue and how many users left the queue

➤ Subject of questions or keywords, as provided by the responding librarian

➤ Number of questions answered in a single interaction

➤ IP ranges or addresses of patron computers

➤ Patron browser and operating system information

➤ Consortium information such as answering library, referrals between libraries, home library of patron, and home library of the answering librarian

These data points provide a lot to work with—maybe more than you need or perhaps not exactly what you want. There are usually preselected reports that can be generated, and there may be the ability to build your own report types. If you want to generate your own reports, you may want the ability to extract the data easily and download it into different software where you can manipulate it.

Of tremendous importance to most libraries is that the information about patrons be stored separately from transcripts in order to maintain privacy and anonymity. This may not be possible with e-mail, since that requires at least the e-mail address for response. Information such as IP address, browser type, and, if required for entry, patron ID should be stored apart from the transcript or not kept at all.

Customizable surveys are often built into commercial software so that the survey can be easily pushed to the patron and the data collected, stored, and analyzed within the same system. There may or may not (most likely not) be a link between the question asked and the survey responses.

If the software you are examining lacks assessment features, it may be possible to work around this by designing other ways to collect data. For instance, a tech-savvy librarian or a member of your IT department may devise a way to collect from the IM transcripts average length of transaction, number of questions answered, traffic patterns by time of day, and so forth.

Consortial Support

Some of the software marketed to libraries, most notably QuestionPoint and Docutek VRLplus, emphasizes support of reference consortia. They have features for group administration such as scheduling, multiple queues for incoming questions, and routing questions (automated and manual). The ability to maintain a library-specific queue and a shared queue is of particular importance to many libraries, so that their patrons are routed to them when they are online and directed to any available librarian when the home library is not staffing the service. These features are unique to library software, since collaboration is not really a factor for businesses and IM is designed toward the needs of individuals rather than groups.

There is more discussion of consortial support in chapter 10. If a consortium is in your future, read that chapter before making your software decisions.

Where to Find Software

Library Sellers

At the writing of this book, there are three major virtual reference software packages marketed specifically to libraries: QuestionPoint (QP) from OCLC, Docutek VRLplus from SirsiDynix, and Live Homework Help and Ask A Librarian from Tutor.com. These vendors are easy to find online and easy to contact during library conferences, where they almost always have booths. They are happy to provide you with material about their products, and you may be able to arrange a short trial to view the librarian and administrative interfaces of their programs. Sometimes it is difficult during a trial to get a good idea of how the software works in production. For instance, it may be difficult to run sample reports unless the vendor has populated the test database with transcripts and log data. Ask for a list of clients near you so that you can visit and view their system from the administrative side and, of course, so that you can receive honest feedback about the product from libraries that use it.

One of the nice aspects of using software marketed to libraries is the community of librarians that surrounds these products. Even if you are not part of a virtual reference consortium, librarians are willing to talk about their experiences. It is also easy to search online mailing list archives like DIG_REF.[4]

Customer Service, Call Management, and Help Desk Software

Other options for providing virtual reference are systems that are not designed for libraries but can be adapted for their use. These include software marketed to call centers (e.g., IT help desks and online retail centers) and enterprise collaboration software.

To find companies offering these products, search the Internet for "enterprise collaboration," "live chat," "customer service software," "contact center software" or "help desk software." Industry changes the hot terms for these services fairly frequently, so if the results you find seem dated talk to your local business librarian. You can also look around at your favorite online retailers and see what product they are using to support the "live chat" feature of their website. This is a less systematic but perhaps faster and more entertaining way to start identifying products.

Why might you look at these products? First, they may already be in use in other parts of your organization (e.g., campus IT help desk or city human resources office), and their license might cover use by the library. Second, they are often very full-featured and may provide more administrative features and communication options than the products marketed to libraries, although they may give you more than you need.

As with software designed for the library market, ask for a trial and list of clients.

Freeware, Shareware, and Open-Source Applications

Some librarians and IT folk like shareware and freeware software solutions because they have low costs, and open-source software allows for collaborative development. Collaborative development means that good products can be improved by others who are willing to share their developments or add-ons with the open-source community. If your library is considering any software options that fall into these categories, definitely bring in your IT department early in your planning, since more of the server hosting and maintenance responsibilities are likely to fall on them. SourceForge (www .sourceforge.net) offers a portal to thousands of open-source applications. Be aware that not all that is open-source is free, and not all that is free is open-source.

The Future of Virtual Reference Software

Predicting the future of software development is tricky. Buff Hirko wrote in 2001, when virtual reference was just starting, "What we can be certain of is continuing change in the type and number of vendors, significant improvements in capability, and unforeseen developments in technology."[5] In the six years since that was written there have been side-by-side trends of using more sophisticated software with co-browsing and collaboration features, and using the much simpler IM software. This trend of development in different directions continues, with some librarians wanting to provide the user with a more "immersive" virtual reference experience complete with audio and video and others embedding small text-only IM widgets into their library web pages. Chapter 14, on emerging technologies, offers some insight into technologies that we may come to use in virtual service to our patrons.

NOTES

1. Ralph Lee Scott, "Wired to the World: Skype," *North Carolina Libraries* 63 (Spring/Summer 2006): 32.
2. David Ward and M. Kathleen Kern, "Combining IM and Vendor-Based Chat: A Report from the Frontlines of an Integrated Service," *Portal: Libraries and the Academy* 6 (October 2006): 417–429.
3. Melissa Records, e-mail to M. K. Kern, March 31, 2007.
4. DIG_REF archives, http://digref.org/archive/. To sign up for this list, see information at www.webjunction.org/do/DisplayContent?id=11740.
5. Buff Hirko, "Live, Digital Reference Marketplace," *Library Journal,* October 15, 2002, www.libraryjournal.com/index.asp?layout=article&articleid=CA251679&publication=libraryjournal.

CHAPTER 7

Communication

DO I HAVE TO LEARN A NEW LANGUAGE?

Communication in virtual reference is an area of some uncertainty and even fear. It is the newest part of the entire endeavor for some librarians.

We are used to learning new software; we are used to communicating with patrons in the reference interview; we know our sources and how to help; but we are not used to learning a new way to communicate. Most people have grown up using the telephone, and e-mail is commonplace enough in the workplace, not to mention socially, to be second nature to librarians who may have not used a computer until many years into their careers. But the idea of "chatting" with a patron through typing rather than voice may be daunting. Where we once felt expert, we now feel like novices. Of course, many librarians use IM to chat with friends or when purchasing things online, so attitudes and comfort levels vary widely.

Before you continue into this chapter, take a few minutes to complete exercise 7-1. After you have read the chapter, determine if any of your answers have changed.

Distribute exercise 7-1 to everyone at your library who will be staffing the virtual reference service. Almost everyone working in reference knows something about IM or online chat; they've used it, attended a program, or read an article. The exercise is a chance to record what they know and how they feel about it and will serve as a starting point for your own conversation about communicating in virtual reference. When I use this exercise, I have had participants in my workshops keep this for themselves—it is not collected—so they can write whatever they want. I do use it to start a discussion of virtual communication, asking them to volunteer to share what they see as different and how they think they might be able to communicate effectively online.

The outcomes of this exercise are

- ➤ Self-discovery by individuals of their thoughts and fears about virtual communication
- ➤ Brainstorming of possible barriers to communication presented by the online environment
- ➤ Generating ideas about how to overcome difficulties in virtual communication and sharing positive experiences of online communication

Perceptions of Virtual Communications

What do you believe *virtual communications* means? Take ten or fifteen minutes to write down what you know and what you feel about online communication. Think about what you have experienced, read, and heard from others. Everyone's responses will be shared with the group, according to instructions given to you by your team leader.

1. How does communication online (via chat/IM) differ from communication in person? From the telephone?

2. What are the challenges of this type of communication? Are there any unique challenges in using this for reference rather than for casual communication between friends?

3. In what ways is online communication better than face-to-face or telephone communication?

4. If you use IM or online chat in your personal life, what elements do you like or dislike about it as a form of communication? Why do you choose to use IM or chat?

5. What can be done to diminish any problems in communication introduced by the online medium?

Style

It is indisputable that online communications have their own unique style elements. Just as the telephone has its conventions—greetings and closings, protocol for placing people on hold, times of day to call—so does the medium of online communication via chat and IM. There are some differences between these two, although there is also overlap, so I refer to them individually and also collectively as *virtual reference* when a style holds true for both.

Speed

There are some expectations of speed in online communications. It is, after all, called "instant" messaging. There is also, somewhat surprisingly, quite a lot of willingness to wait for a response. There are ways to strike a balance between speedy communications and the time you need to find an answer or locate a source.

Communicating to the patron that you need time to search and providing an approximate length of time that she will be on hold are essential. Responding to the patron within that window is important, even if it is to only say that you are still looking. Otherwise, the patron may come to the conclusion that she is forgotten or that you have gone to lunch. This is very much like placing a telephone patron on hold. How long are people willing to be on hold listening to "Hooked on Classics 4" or, worse, silence? From my experience, two minutes is about as long as you should go without communicating something to the virtual patron. If you need to walk into another room to consult a source, let the patron know that and ask if she can wait five minutes or however long it will take. If it seems appropriate, or the patron indicates that she cannot wait, ask if she would like you to reply by e-mail or phone with a response.

This willingness to wait online comes from the multitasking that patrons do while online. It is not uncommon for people to be talking via IM to more than one friend at once. They may also be in the middle of writing a paper and pausing to do a bit of research, so they can continue writing while they wait, or open a new window to check their e-mail. There are innumerable online and offline computer activities that can occupy a patron while waiting for your response. Just remember to communicate well about time expectations and not leave the patron hanging.

Typing—Short Is Sweet

Central to the speed of communication is the brevity of online responses and disregard of certain conventions of written communication. Do not write paragraphs. I try to avoid "don'ts," but this one is really important. If you are composing a paragraph, the patron is waiting the entire time that you are typing. Frequently, though, a paragraph or long sentence is needed. In such cases, rather than typing everything and then sending it, break your response into shorter segments of text. Ellipses are useful for indicating that you have more to say, so that the patron does not assume you are done with your response. For example:

> *Patron:* How do find a book at the library?
>
> *Librarian:* Do you have a specific book you need?

Patron: yes, Tom Sawyer

Librarian: ok, from the library's homepage: www.library.uiuc.edu . . .

Librarian: click on the link for "online catalog," then . . .

Librarian: type in the title and select "title" from the pull-down menu . . .

In this way, a list of instructions can be broken up to supply a more constant stream of communications. Given the format of most IM and chat windows, it is also easier to read than sending an entire block of text, which would look something like this:

> *Librarian:* Let me make sure that I understand this, you are looking for articles on dairy farming and bovine growth hormone in Great Britain that were written within the past five years? You also need some scholarly perspectives as well as some editorials from major newspapers?

This text looks dense and is difficult to read quickly in a small window. Notice that it also does not give the patron a chance to interject if some element is wrong. Breaking up what you have to say (or ask) facilitates the reference interview process. It also makes you seem more friendly in that it reads more like an invitation to conversation than a librarian giving a speech to the patron.

Grammar

Much to the dismay of defenders of good grammar and punctuation, people using chat and IM are a bit loose with their grammatical style. Capitalization is often abandoned in favor of typing speed. Typos go uncorrected for the same reason. Punctuation in particular tends to go by the wayside or be reduced to ellipses. Functionally, clauses are often indicated by a line break (much like some poetry) rather than by commas.

Grammar is less a victim than punctuation. Naomi Baron has studied college students' use of IM and found that "the misspellings, the shortcuts . . . just weren't there in the way you'd expect."[1] College-age patrons are more aware of nuances of formality and communicate differently in online communications when they know that the communication is of a business or work nature. The same cannot always be expected of preteens and teenagers, who, according to Baron, use language (including IM communication) as a "marker of in-group status." The younger users are much less formal with all of their online communications and use slang and style to determine how "in" other people are. This is not to say that librarians need to adopt all the latest slang to reach these users, and they may be called out as fake if they do, but expectations of formality should be adjusted when serving these users groups.

Abbreviations and Lingo

Knowledge of common abbreviations is good, but for the reasons stated above most virtual reference services do not encounter a lot of them, particularly with college audiences. It is common for libraries to keep a list of Internet abbreviations and slang at the service desk when they first start the service but to remove it when it is clear that it is not needed, either through lack of use or staff familiarity. It is also relatively easy to find guides to these online, and, after all, we are reference librarians.

As far as librarians using abbreviations and such, this is a matter of personal style and preference. The only rule is to not be less formal than your patron; let the patron set the tone.

Personal Style

Just as everyone has a personal style of speech, they also have personal styles of written communication. Your own style is likely to come through in online communications, and this is perfectly acceptable. This helps to make the librarian more approachable and to create a conversational connection with the user. But do not let personal style trump good online practices. Here are some good rules to follow:

➤ Keep communication going—avoid long periods of online "silence."
➤ Let the patron set the tone for formality.
➤ Send text in small fragments.

Aside from these principles, let as much personality show as you like. Displaying your personality lets the patron know that you are not a robot. If your patron makes a joke, it is okay to laugh. Let the communication be as natural online as it is on the telephone or face to face.

Making Up for Lack of Visual/Vocal

One of the things that scares librarians about online communications is the lack of visual or verbal aids. We are used to the richer communication media of the telephone and face-to-face interactions, where we can more easily tell if the user is confused or understands. Absence of vocal inflection and facial expression cannot be made up for in the "thin" communication of IM and e-mail. At least not yet. There are methods for communicating to mitigate the thinness of the online media. Marie Radford has done much excellent research in this area, and the techniques of inclusion and self-disclosure are from her studies.[2] Later in this chapter, Lena Singer summarizes the key points from one of Radford's articles in a Research You Can Use.

Approachability

Approachability online begins before you have greeted the patron. Like the in-person reference desk and the demeanor of the person staffing it, your web page sets the tone for your online service. The look of your library's website as a whole is critical, but since the reference staff's influence on the overall look of the website may be limited, focus on the pages that you can design. There should be one web page that serves as the home page or entry point for all of a library's online services. I prefer a page that draws together all the online and offline ways to reach the library. This way, the patron sees all options at once and can make the most informed decisions. Considerations for this page are clarity, attractiveness, and welcoming:

Clarity. Is the purpose of the web page immediately obvious? Does the eye know where to go? This is particularly important if you are presenting multiple options for communication. Can the patron easily determine which information belongs with which service? Can she distinguish the hours for the IM service from the hours for walk-in assistance? Not all information needs to be on the home page for the service, but it should be clear where to go for more about policies, who staffs the service, and other common topics.

Attractiveness.   There is likely to be an overall approved look for library web pages. Work within this so that the patron can easily identify the virtual reference service as part of the library. Pay attention as you lay out your page to white space, which serves to make a document appear less crowded and more readable.

Welcoming.   Static as they are, web pages can be welcoming. The text of the web page reflects an attitude about the service. Are you inviting people to ask questions or subtly turning them away? There is a difference between saying "Your question is important to us; sometimes you will need to wait for a reply while we assist other patrons," and "Librarians are here to assist you with your research. Sometimes a lot of people need our help. We will be with you as quickly as we can." Notice that the first example uses "you" more and the second uses "we" more, placing the emphasis on the responsibility of the librarian and less on the patron.

The last factor in being approachable online is to be ubiquitous—everywhere at once. Place a link to your service prominently and on as many library web pages as possible. A link in your library's banner or sidebar that appears on every library web page is best. This is prime website real estate and everyone wants it, but a patron needing help should be a top concern. Many libraries have links to their virtual reference service within their online catalogs and subscription databases. These are fantastic examples of point-of-need assistance.

Greeting

Just as with the other forms of communication, an online greeting sets the tone for the conversation. Avoid sounding robotic. Canned messages are a fast way to send text, so many libraries use a standard greeting. I find that it is just as quick to type, "Hello, how may I help you?" and it leaves room for me to vary the greeting. This spontaneity spills over into the rest of my interaction. With IM, and sometimes with chat, it is the patron who makes the first communication and initiates the conversation. Pay attention to the formality of the patron's greeting and let that guide you.

Fight the desire to collect information about the patron immediately. It may be important to your service that you know if the patron is a resident of your town or a student at your university, but it should not be the first thing you ask; it will sound abrupt. Ask first for the patron's question, and then establish other things that you might need to know as part of the reference interview. This emphasizes that your first concern is with the question and that status, location, and the like are necessary but secondary. Of course, if you do not need this information, avoid asking and save your time and the user's.

Sometimes the patron launches into a question without the nicety of a "hello." This may or may not indicate that the patron is in a hurry. It is possible that the patron is not familiar with online communication. It may also indicate a nonnative speaker of English (or the language of your service). It may be that the patron has recently communicated with the library online and thinks that you are the same librarian who assisted her earlier. Greet the patron anyway, and then get on with the question. This is another good reason to not use canned greetings—you look silly or inattentive to ask "How may I help you?" if the patron has already asked a question.

Being Friendly in Cyberspace

There are a variety of emoticons (symbols such as smiley faces) to communicate emotion in online communications. Generally, do not use an emoticon unless the patron has done so first. If your patron sends an emoticon first, then you know that this is something with which they are familiar and consider appropriate to use with the librarian. Emoticons can be useful not only to display friendliness but to diffuse a situation in which the patron has been confused or the librarian has made a mistake.

Another way to be friendly is to reveal your humanness. Even if your personal style tends toward formal, you can avoid being robotic or stiff. Do not sweat every piece of punctuation and do not try to craft perfect prose. Strive for clarity and brevity. The lengthy paragraph is distancing.

Include your patron in the search process. This not only takes advantage of a teachable moment to instruct the user in research but also makes the user a full participant in the conversation. Conversely, include yourself in the search process. When you send instructions about how to search, use "we" instead of "you." Say "Let's search the online catalog. We'll start at the library's homepage ..." rather than "You need to search the online catalog. Go to the library's homepage ..." Instructions that say "you" are an online equivalent to pointing. They will get the job done of telling the patron where to go, but they are not as friendly. Make the patron aware that you are there by his side, working on the same question.

Make Contact

I really cannot say this enough. Short of avoiding rudeness, contact is the most important part of online communication. Without verbal or visual contact, the only way the patron knows where you are is for you to tell him. Do not leave the patron hanging in cyberspace. Communicate how long it will be before you return, and if the information proves difficult to find and you need more time let the patron know. It also can be helpful to add such language as "This is more difficult to find than I thought," "I am helping two people. It is a busy night, but I am working on your question," or "I've found the right place to look, now I need to do some searching."

If you are searching with the patron, make contact to confirm that the patron is doing fine with the search and the instructions you have sent. In this case, you may be waiting for a reply from the patron, but he is unlikely to know that. Ask "Do you see the search box?" "Does this make sense?" or "I found twenty articles with that search. How many do you have?"—whatever is appropriate for the search process in which you are involved. This keeps the librarian in contact with the patron and ensures that the patron does not get too lost in the instructions. It also gives the patron a good opportunity to let you know that he has found what he needs. When I see two-hour online

Encountering Virtual Users:
A Qualitative Investigation of Interpersonal Communication in Chat Reference

Marie Radford, Rutgers School of Communication, Information and Library Studies, *Journal of the American Society for Information Science and Technology* 57, no. 8 (2006): 1046–1059.

Of the research studies that have been conducted on virtual reference to date, most have focused on the efficiency and accuracy of the answers librarians provide through chat, IM, or other real-time virtual reference services.

Marie Radford's 2006 study of chat reference was one of the first to examine qualitatively the interpersonal—or "relational"—behaviors of patrons and librarians during virtual reference interactions and to apply a theoretical perspective—in this case, communication theory—to that evaluation.

Previous studies have shown that the interpersonal aspects of a reference interview—saying hello and goodbye to the patron, for example—are central to patrons' perceptions of a service. Radford set out to determine whether the same was true for the online reference environment by examining the interpersonal communication in chat transcripts.

Radford found that many of the interpersonal cues that are important in face-to-face reference interactions are just as key to the virtual reference experience. Using communication theory as her framework, she was able to identify common "relational facilitators" and "relational barriers" within the two groups of transcripts.

Relational facilitators—interpersonal signals that had a positive impact on virtual reference interviews—included actions (on the part of the librarian) like offering a greeting at the beginning of the interaction, making an effort to build rapport, compensating for a lack of nonverbal cues (e.g., with emoticons or well-selected punctuation), showing deference to a patron's own experience, and successfully closing the interview with a friendly goodbye.

Among the relational barriers—aspects that had a negative effect on interviews—were failure to build rapport, ending a chat without saying goodbye, or bringing a chat to a close by using a negative strategy (basically, by ending with something other than a helpful answer or words of farewell).

Although the interpersonal skills that enhance the traditional reference interview won't translate exactly to online environments (e.g., the use of visual cues), Radford's study shows that online reference is, in fact, "no less personal than face-to-face."

Summary by Lena Singer

conversations in a library's reports on its traffic, I wonder how many of these are improperly closed reference interviews with the librarian waiting for the patron to indicate closure.

Self-Disclosure

The reference interview is a formal interaction rather than a casual conversation. Just how formal depends on the library setting and the librarian, but there are conventions and expectations for this type of communication, just as there are when talking with a physician about your health or an accountant about your taxes. It is a mistake, however, to equate this type of formality with rigidity or lack of personality. Level of comfort with another person, particularly in a professional setting, depends upon feeling that you know an appropriate amount about the other person to determine that they are sincere, nonjudgmental, knowledgeable, and trustworthy. In the absence of visual cues or vocal inflection, self-disclosure can create this rapport. So, if a patron reveals that she feels stupid because she finds the library's website difficult to use, do not ignore this comment. Acknowledge it by saying something like "We have a big website, so it can be confusing," or "I'm sorry that the website isn't easy, but that's why I'm here." You can even throw in your own self-disclosure, such as acknowledging that you are finding a piece of information more difficult to uncover than expected.

Difficult Communications

Sometimes communication is difficult. This is true in person and via telephone and is not unique to chat. Patrons may be frustrated or angry, though without pushing the boundaries of abuse. These patrons need to be handled with politeness and professionalism. Marie Radford and Joe Thompson provide a good list of recommendations for dealing with rude and impatient patrons in virtual reference: see figure 7-1.[3]

Then there are the patrons who are not rude but may not be seen as using the service as it is intended. Rick Roche of the Thomas Ford Memorial Library in Illinois has a good approach to these situations:

> Sometimes we do attract a client without questions—somebody just wanting to chat about nothing in particular. Regular clients who come to the building sometimes want to do the same thing at the reference desk. It seems to me like a way to reach out and connect, so I have no problem with just chatting for a minute or so.[4]

The Medium Does Not Change the Message

Be the same in your goals. Don't let perceived (or real) pressure change the service offered. The virtual patron is as important as the in-person patron. I learned this quite early in my career. At 8:30 at night a graduate student contacted the library via our new chat reference service. His reference question was fairly substantive and taking more time than we typically spent with online patrons at that time. At one point he asked me to hold. I was puzzled but said yes. He thanked me because he was at home and had to take his three-year old daughter to the bathroom. He was very appreciative

FIGURE 7-1 RECOMMENDATIONS FOR VIRTUAL REFERENCE ENCOUNTERS WITH RUDE OR IMPATIENT CLIENTS

Remember that you have skills and experience in dealing with rude/impatient people in face-to-face encounters. These skills can be just as effective in virtual encounters.

➤ Use your common sense, intuition, and experience to defuse problematic encounters.

When users are impatient ("Hurry, hurry!"), let them know realistically how long you think that the search for the needed information will take.

➤ If you estimate that it will take more than a minute or so, tell them and ask if they are willing to wait (e.g., "I know you are in a hurry, but this search will take about 4 to 5 minutes. Can you wait?")

➤ Presenting a realistic estimate of the time needed may prevent abrupt user departures.

➤ If they can't wait, apologize and present an alternative (e.g., I'm sorry I can't answer your question quickly, but I can e-mail that answer to you within 2–3 days).

➤ During the time users are waiting while you search, check in occasionally and give a quick update like "still searching. . . ." Periodic reassurances will also prevent abrupt departures.

Do not "mirror" rude behavior; this only provokes more rudeness.

Be polite and professional at all times.

Resist the urge to reprimand or admonish users for rude behavior or FLAMING, again this only provokes more rude behavior.

Avoid jargon or language that will create a barrier or send the message that you are blindly following the rule book.

Apologize to the user as appropriate; this does not mean that you are accepting the blame.

➤ An apology can diffuse potentially rude behavior (e.g., "I'm sorry that you had to wait so long; our service is very busy today" or, "I'm sorry that I can't help with your request this time; please visit your local library for that information.").

If the user complains about library service or another librarian, thank them for bringing their concern to your attention and promise to follow-up.

➤ Regard a complaint as a gift, as a way to improve service.

Do not be condescending to a person with a "simple question." Sometimes parents are helping their children with homework and you may insult them. Treat all users with equal courtesy and respect.

Realize that rude or impatient users are in the minority, but understand that you will encounter one now and then.

➤ Your polite response to them instructs them on how to use the service properly in the future.

Do not take rude behavior personally. Users may be stressed by deadlines or other life problems and their rudeness and impatience usually have nothing to do with you or your service.

Reprinted from *The Virtual Reference Desk: Creating a Virtual Future* with permission of Neal-Schuman Publishers. This excerpt © 2007 by Marie Radford; compilation © 2007 by Neal-Schuman Publishers.

of the new virtual service. I decided this was the perfect counter to librarians who thought virtual reference was a second-class service; here was a hardworking, on-campus student who we saved from dragging his tired toddler with him in order to work in the evening.

Practice and Review

Practice is really the only way to become familiar with online communications and the online reference interview in particular. See chapter 11 for some practice questions. Keep in mind these basic points while you practice, and review your performance by looking at the transcripts, or reflecting on the experience, when you are done:

> ➤ Keep sentences short. Fragments are fine and ellipses are helpful.
> ➤ Most virtual patrons are friendly—probably in about the same proportions as those in person. Dispose of preconceptions that online patrons are more impatient or demanding.
> ➤ Type with speed and do not worry too much about punctuation or grammar.
> ➤ The reference interview is as important online as it is face to face.
> ➤ Keep in constant communication—no more than two minutes without communicating.
> ➤ Be friendly. You are a person, not a robot.

NOTES

1. Naomi S. Baron, "Instant Messaging by American College Students: A Case Study in Computer-Mediated Communication," presented at the American Association for the Advancement of Science annual meeting, Washington, DC, February 17–21, 2005, www.american.edu/tesol/Baron-AAAS-IM%20by%20American%20 College%20Students.pdf.
2. Marie L. Radford, "Encountering Virtual Users: A Qualitative Investigation of Interpersonal Communication in Chat Reference," *Journal of the American Society for Information Science and Technology* 57, no. 8 (2006): 1046–1059. See also Marie L. Radford, "Encountering Users: Applying Interpersonal Communication Theory in the Library Context," *Journal of Education for Library and Information Science* 42, no. 1 (2001): 27–41.
3. Marie Radford, " Investigating Interpersonal Communication in Chat Reference: Dealing with Impatient Users and Rude Encounters," in *The Virtual Reference Desk: Creating a Reference Future,* ed. R. David Lankes et al. (New York: Neal-Schuman, 2004); also presented at the Virtual Reference Desk 6th Annual Conference, Cincinnati, OH, November 8–9, 2004, as Marie Radford and Joseph Thompson, "Yo Dude! Y R U Typin So Slow? Interpersonal Communication in Chat Reference Encounters," http://data.webjunction.org/wj/documents/ 12497.pdf.
4. Rick Roche, e-mail to M. K. Kern, March 1, 2007.

CHAPTER 8

Determining
a Staffing Model

One of the biggest challenges in writing the VR Guidelines was giving meaningful guidance without being overprescriptive. Nowhere was this tension more evident than in the area of staffing.

Some librarians quite fervently believed that the VR Guidelines should state that virtual reference (chat particularly) must be staffed away from the public service desk—that it was inappropriate to staff it from a desk that also accepted in-person questions. Other librarians noted that the only way they could offer virtual reference would be to staff it from their reference desk; these included librarians from single-librarian libraries as well as some from larger libraries who were already staffing virtual service from their reference desk. There is no evidence that size or type of library requires a particular model of staffing.

Ultimately, the statement in the guidelines on staffing models became "Each library should examine staffing models to determine one that is appropriate for their organization. While there is not a 'one-size-fits-all' service model, a model should be chosen which would support quality reference interactions via all modes of communication" (see appendix A). This is a short statement for an issue this complex and central to the operation of the service, but given the variance in librarian opinion on this matter, the committee felt it inappropriate to dictate such an organizationally dependent issue.

If staffing can be a contentious issue among a group of librarians from different organizations, it has the potential to be a knotty issue at your library as well. At my library, the University of Illinois at Urbana Central Reference department, we were perhaps fortunate enough to have started our service so early that there were no services to model ourselves after. There were also no self-proclaimed experts offering opinions on how we should staff. We chose a model and decided to try it. It was based on some practical discussions and what seemed like it might work best within the staffing model we used for our reference service. The decision was also influenced by our collaboration with the undergraduate library.

This is not to say that all of our librarians were totally comfortable with the staffing model chosen, at the outset. Eventually we all decided that it worked for us but that we would need to review the efficacy of our chosen model periodically.

Unless you flipped to this chapter first, you probably suspect that I am going to suggest a process for making a decision relevant to your own library's needs. First, however, I arm you with some information for making a decision. I identify three major staffing models. Figure 8-1 summarizes the pros and cons of these models.

Staffing Models

Staffing All Services from One Desk

In this model, the library staffs all reference services from a single, public service point. The "one desk" model encompasses all modes of communication—face to face, telephone, chat, and e-mail (as well as any other way that you might communicate with your patrons, e.g., videoconferencing, telepathy).

During the early years of virtual reference, many librarians (both those doing and those not doing virtual reference) voiced the opinion that it was not appropriate to staff synchronous virtual reference from the reference desk. As virtual reference has matured, this thinking has changed. For some libraries, this is the only way to staff virtual reference service. Why this is the case is obvious for small libraries with only one or two staff members. Other libraries find it an efficient use of resources that works with their reference workflow.

Answering all questions from the same desk minimizes downtime between patrons (particularly if your reference statistics have been declining but your staffing has stayed consistent). Peak times for virtual reference may be different from the peak times of your in-person service, staggering your

FIGURE 8-1 THREE STAFFING MODELS: PROS AND CONS

Model	Pros	Cons
One desk	➤ May use existing staffing levels ➤ Increase utilization of staff at desk ➤ Proximity of print resources ➤ Advertising of all services	➤ Librarian overload ➤ Juggling patrons/multiple questions ➤ May require additional staffing to meet demands on service
Separate virtual desk	➤ Less juggling of patrons ➤ More dedicated time for each individual user ➤ Decreased librarian burnout	➤ Requires additional staffing ➤ May have idle periods, both for in-person desk and remote desk ➤ May need to duplicate a few print resources
Staff from librarians' offices	➤ Same as the "virtual desk" option, plus . . . ➤ Does not require additional staff ➤ Decreases librarian idle time if service not busy	➤ Less uninterrupted time for other work ➤ Must be recognized as "desk time" and scheduled ➤ Librarian may be distracted, resentful ➤ No print resources

influx of questions. To make a parallel that appears often in this book, staffing chat or IM as an additional mode of communication at the reference desk has the same advantages (and disadvantages) as answering the telephone from the reference desk. Many libraries staff their telephone reference service from their "in-person" reference desk. In fact, most libraries do not even think of telephone reference as a separate service (New York Public being one notable exception).

Even in the age of digital information, print reference works are sometimes still needed to answer virtual questions. By answering all reference questions from the same location, you ensure easy access to print reference works. This could ease some anxiety for staff who are reluctant to place themselves in an all-electronic situation.

One of the biggest sources of reluctance regarding answering virtual reference questions from the reference desk is patron perception. A librarian busy typing to a remote patron may seem unapproachable to an in-person patron. But since the remote patron cannot see or hear the in-person patron, the librarian can greet the in-person patron without really interrupting the online communication that is in progress. This may be awkward for librarians to learn, and patrons need to be made aware that you are assisting another patron—since this is not as obvious as when you are talking on the telephone. This is where explaining to an in-person patron that you are helping a patron online can become advertising for your virtual reference service. This juggling of virtual and in-person patrons may raise issues of which patron should take priority, in-person or online. This is a policy issue, discussed in chapter 5. Additionally, good communication is a key to a courteous online presence when working with simultaneous patrons in various modes of communication.

The difficulty with the one-desk model is really one of juggling multiple patrons—something that already happens at busy reference desks with multiple in-person or telephone patrons. It may be a situation that the librarians are uncomfortable with initially, particularly if their level of comfort with the software is low, or if the demand at the desk is greatly increased by the addition of virtual reference questions. If you have a constant flow of questions, your present staffing levels may not be able to absorb the increase caused by virtual reference questions. This could negate the primary cost-savings benefit of answering virtual reference questions from the reference desk.

Workload and staff comfort are important considerations; if staff feel pressured because of the volume of questions or too many types of communication, decline in service quality or staff burnout may result. It is important, then, to have a discussion about staffing models that includes a wide cross section of the staff. If your library's reference staff is not too large, everyone can be part of the decision making for choosing a staffing model. Exercise 8-1 provides a framework for the discussion of staffing models. Don't skip ahead to the exercise yet, though; there are still two more staffing models to consider.

The Library Field Report from Melissa Records encapsulates the benefits and stresses of staffing all reference services from one desk.

Staffing Virtual Reference at a Mid-size Public Library

For the most part at Champaign Public Library, we monitor instant messages (and chat, e-mail, phone, and in person) out at the reference desk, although it can be monitored from anywhere. The person who is the reference librarian usually logs in at the computer that he or she is likely to spend the most time at (we tend to get up and move around a lot when at the desk). We basically listen for incoming IM messages (we have speakers and sound cards on all of our computers) the same way we listen for incoming phone calls. We do sometimes monitor IM in the staff workroom, but it really doesn't add much to the load at the reference desk and it fits there best functionally—that is where we deal with reference questions. If you are monitoring in the workroom, you're sort of stuck at your computer.

Things improved quite a lot when we got sound and speakers on our computers. We no longer had to be sitting in front of our computers *watching* for incoming chat and IM. We could just be nearby them and hear the incoming calls. This change made things easier for all of us. The downside of using sound is that you *do* get a lot of different sounds—sounds from your computer's programs, sounds from people logging in and out of their IM accounts, and more. That takes some getting used to, but you eventually learn to identify the sounds that mean actual incoming reference questions and ignore the other sounds.

We might have to change staffing models when we get into our new library building (which is three times the size of our current building) this fall. For now, the downside of monitoring at the public service desk is that it is yet one more thing to pay attention to—a not insignificant problem since it gets to be an overload on busy days. I personally find it very distracting to have to pay attention to chat, e-mail, IM, phone, and in-person interactions as well as having eyes in the back of my head to watch middle school students and other interesting characters.

We were concerned that patrons would think we were typing on the computer and ignoring them. Usually, if an IM question is in session when an in-person patron comes in, we just inform that patron that we have someone "on the line," so to speak. No one has seemed fazed or put out by this.

Instant messaging is just one more thing on the plate. It doesn't require a lot of time, but keeping track of one more type of incoming question is stressful for staff.

Melissa Records, Champaign Public Library, Champaign, Illinois

Staffing Virtual Reference from a "Virtual Desk"

The obvious alternative to staffing all services from the reference desk is to staff virtual reference from somewhere else. There are a couple of different ways that this can be arranged. One option is to establish a separate "virtual desk." This can be located near the in-person desk to take advantage of print materials and ease communication with the rest of the reference staff. The disadvantage is that, if the librarian is visible to walk-up patrons, then he will need to assist them. Alternately, a library may have an available "consultation room" or empty office near the reference desk that would have the advantage of proximity to staff and collections but the added benefit of quiet and separation from walk-up patrons, allowing the librarian to concentrate solely on virtual reference questions. The most significant drawback to this model is that it requires extra scheduling and probably extra staff since it requires an additional service point. There will be an economic gain, or at least a breakeven, if the creation of a separate desk results in staffing fewer librarians at the in-person desk.

Another option with the "virtual desk" is to have it handle all remote communication, including telephone as well as e-mail and chat/IM. Whether this is advisable depends on the volume of questions received through the telephone. Other combinations are possible, such as the in-person desk performing triage for telephone questions and transferring more complicated questions to the "virtual desk."

This separate-desk model is employed by the New York Public Library, which has maintained a separate telephone service since 1968. Some other large public libraries use this same model, and it is possible that volume is part of the economics of maintaining a separate telephone and virtual reference desk.

For New York Public, at least, the addition of virtual reference to the telephone reference center's workflow has filled the gap of declining telephone inquiries. "While the number of telephone calls has declined over the years to fewer than 150 a day from more than 1,000, they still made up two-thirds, or 41,715, of all inquiries to the staff last year (the rest were by computer)." It should be noted, though, that there is little information available that would help determine when to staff a telephone desk. Because New York Public telephone inquiries are limited to five minutes but virtual inquiries are not (acknowledging that this form of communication can take more time), the virtual inquiries take 85 percent of the staff's time.[1]

Staffing Virtual Reference from Nondesk Locations

A second way to staff away from the main reference desk is something of a variation on the "virtual desk." Some libraries staff virtual reference with librarians who are working in their own offices or from home. Laptops could allow this work to be done from any location. Librarians may also work on other tasks unrelated to answering patron inquiries during these shifts, and this is seen as one of the advantages of this model. There is a cost savings because there is no additional dedicated staff for virtual reference. This arrangement does bring with it some different issues, so it merits its own discussion.

The flip side to the cost savings is that, even though there is not additional librarian time dedicated exclusively to virtual reference, it is still taking time away from other responsibilities.

Librarians are limited in the work they can accomplish during their scheduled virtual reference shifts since they cannot work on projects that require uninterrupted time. It may be a source of frustration to be working in your own office but unable to complete the same types of tasks as during unscheduled time.

Librarians have also voiced dismay over this model when they felt that this additional shift was not recognized as added work. This can also be a problem with the "virtual desk" model, but it seems to be more of a complaint when the "offices" model is used. Staffing from offices can create the assumption from management that there is no additional work and no impact on the librarians' other responsibilities. So, the flexibility afforded by this model is appreciated, but the lack of recognition is not. Workload needs to be adjusted accordingly or more flexibility allowed elsewhere. This is important for management to keep in mind so that morale does not fall.

The University of Florida Libraries allows librarians to staff from their homes during some of the virtual reference service hours. This can be a benefit compared to traveling to work in the evening to staff a desk. If librarians are to work from home, certain things must be in place, such as computer and Internet connections, and the library should probably provide these or pick up the cost of work use if these are librarian-provided resources. As with staffing from offices, this time must be acknowledged as work time so that it does not cut into the "life" part of the work-life equation.

Writing in 2003, Jana Ronan presented a wide range of libraries that make full use of the advantages of librarians staffing from offices:

> In this type of organization, librarians may work from a variety of locations: in the same library building; in branch libraries on the same campus or across a city; or across several counties, cities, states, and even countries. For example, at UF [University of Florida], librarians from eight branch libraries work out of their offices and homes. On rare occasions, when short of staff, staff members also work at the reference desk. . . . Some libraries make use of time zones when staffing their services. The Boeing Company's Ask a Librarian service opens with the librarians at the St. Louis location in the morning, and then moves to librarians in Arizona, California, and Puget Sound as the day progresses.[2]

Other Staffing Considerations

Staffing in Consortia

Consortia must decide how they will staff the collaborative service (see chapter 10.) However, each library must also decide internally how it will provide staffing for the hours it covers the consortial queue.

There are several ways that being part of a consortium can affect staffing at the local level:

> ➤ Local libraries staff days and share off-hours staffing with other libraries or contract employees. This allows a local queue to be staffed when the library is open, or during the hours of local virtual reference service, and when the library is closed questions go to a group queue.

➤ All hours of operation are shared between libraries. This results in few hours of staffing each week for each library. It also decreases the likelihood that a librarian will assist her own local patrons.

➤ Each library staffs its own queue and overflow questions are shared. When the local service is busy, questions can roll over to other libraries or contract staff.

➤ Individual libraries staff their own queues but have an option to forward questions (live or e-mail) to subject specialists. This is the model that my large academic library uses; questions come to the central reference and undergraduate libraries and are forwarded to the more specialized libraries when the expertise is required.

Being part of a consortium does alleviate the need for a local decision about who and where you should staff. Your library still needs to determine whether to staff all reference services from one desk, staff virtual reference from a separate desk, or staff it from remote offices.

Who Will Staff the Service

Some libraries have tried to staff with strictly volunteer staff—that is, librarians volunteer to staff the virtual reference service, they staff away from the main reference desk (usually from their offices), and the service is not considered part of their regular reference responsibilities. Verbal reports from librarians who have experienced this model are that staffing a virtual reference service with volunteers is not a sound or stable idea. With volunteers, participation can dwindle and leave all of the hours to a few dedicated, but exhausted, employees. I encourage you to discard the thought.

At some libraries, librarians can opt in or opt out of being part of virtual reference services. Unlike "volunteers," time spent providing virtual reference is recognized as reference service. This model is used to allow reluctant staff (and perhaps their supervisors) an easy way out. It also opens the way for more enthusiastic staff to take a bigger role in virtual reference while acknowledging that they are using time to provide this service. Recalcitrant librarians can result in lower morale among all staff and poor service to your patrons.

Where there are many reference librarians, it is possible to make a call for the number needed to cover the service and allow other librarians to concentrate on other responsibilities. There is an added advantage to limiting the number of librarians involved: too many involved librarians with too few hours staffing virtual reference can lead to lack of proficiency with the software and communication style. It is advisable that every librarian involved in the service staff virtual reference (whether on the desk or off) for at least three hours a week, and with more hours will come more facility.

The downside to opt in/opt out is that it sets up the virtual reference service as separate and auxiliary. It can also create low morale if staff see it as unfair that some activities are optional for some but not others. Thinking about this in terms of an integrated view of reference service, would your library allow public services staff to opt in/opt out of working at the reference desk? If some librarians are allowed (or required) to opt out of providing virtual reference, then achieving balance requires a rebalancing of both reference and nonreference responsibilities across the staff.

Scheduling/Time Accounting

Staffing—who, how, where—are questions that can stall a library wanting to move forward with a new service. Staff costs are the biggest monetary investment for a virtual reference service. Even if no new staff are hired to support the service, time spent staffing the virtual reference service should be figured into cost of operation. With most staffing models, time spent providing virtual reference means time not spent on other responsibilities, and libraries must account for (and plan for) this shift in work.

Someone will need to be in charge of scheduling, of course. If librarians are staffing virtual reference away from the in-person desk, it may be useful, at least at the beginning, to have the scheduler check online to make sure that librarians have remembered their shifts. Even on-desk, checking that the service is logged into is a good idea. It can take some time for this to become part of the routine of staffing.

When to Staff

There are different camps around the when-to-staff decision. There are the librarians who advise a 24/7 live service and say that anything less will result in lower overall use. They contend that 24/7 is the only way patrons will know when to expect service. At the other extreme are librarians who believe that staffing only a few hours a week is vastly better than not offering virtual reference at all.

Not all libraries can manage or afford 24/7, even within a consortium, and not all libraries want to be part of a consortium, so the reality is that 24/7 for all libraries is quite a lofty goal. Consortia have had success with the live 24/7 model, and it certainly does extend the traditional reference service not only into new communication media but also into hours not previously available. This is undeniably a positive development. As for it being a necessity—one without which a service is doomed to fail—a look at the major proponents of the open-all-hours model reveals that some of them are involved with services that provide contracted after-hours service. When reading or listening to an expert, know the source and be wary of those giving advice where there is monetary or job-related gain. Consider also if the speaker has ever worked at a library without a 24/7 service and has any experience with other staffing models. It is good advice in general to seek those with wide-ranging experience or to find balance by talking with librarians from varied institutions and service models.

Very few libraries can afford to hire their own librarians to staff a late-night or 24-hour service. Most libraries wishing to staff extended hours join a consortium to achieve this benefit. The cost of adding librarians to extend hours is more than many libraries can afford on their own. If after-hours volume is sufficient to warrant the cost, then an argument for funding can be made. If your library hires late-night librarians, look for what other work these people can do to provide themselves more balanced and interesting work, particularly at times when the traffic is slow, and to maximize the benefit to the library as well.

As I mentioned earlier in the book, 24/7 should refer only to hours of live assistance, since the ability to send an e-mail or leave a voice message at any time is probably nothing new, and if you cannot expect a reply for hours, then it really is not help at any time of day.

Offering only a few hours of service, on the other hand, can be difficult to market and difficult for patrons to remember. Operating a couple of evenings and a couple of afternoons is unlikely to attract much attention or reference inquiry volume. Just as libraries try to establish some uniformity in their building and reference hours, the same should be done with virtual reference. The staffing model chosen affects the number of hours the service can be offered, since staff can be the largest cost of operating a virtual reference service.

Instant messaging may allow more flexibility with hours. For example, librarians at the Thomas Ford Public Library staff IM from their offices and log in whenever they are available. This flies in the face of conventional virtual reference wisdom, but since this is how patrons log into IM themselves it may fit with their expectations. Rick Roche of Thomas Ford says, "We're sort of on and off, just like the kids are."[3] An icon on the library's website shows patrons if a librarian is available for virtual reference.

Which hours of operation will be most advantageous to your patrons is the fundamental issue, combined with what your library can manage. Some libraries find that their virtual reference services are busiest when their in-person and telephone service is also busiest. This can cause a crunch for staffing but may also mean that late-night hours are not needed. At my academic library, afternoons are busiest for all of our services. Our undergraduate library is a bit different and experiences heavy afternoon volume and another spike in activity around 9:00 p.m. We are not alone. Matt Bejune and Jane Kinkus at Purdue University report similar patterns for virtual and in-person inquiries.[4] Public libraries sometimes see their traffic rise after school and fall off at dinner time. Examining the hours when patrons are using your library web pages, electronic course reserves, and online resources can help you determine optimal hours for virtual reference. Since virtual patrons are often using online resources, this approach to determining hours makes sense. Your IT department may have these statistics on hand or be able to generate a report on request.

Libraries must work within their reality, and if a library can manage only four hours a week, then it may need to examine its staffing model or the overall viability of its service. Joining a consortium may be a way to afford more consistent and robust hours of operation.

Making a Decision on Staffing

Staffing is one of the core decisions in implementing a virtual reference service. Everyone answering your virtual reference questions is affected by the staffing model and should be comfortable with the decision made. It will help everyone to understand the model chosen if they are all brought into the decision process and aware of the factors involved.

Figure 8-1 synopsizes the three staffing models presented in this chapter. Each staff member should have a copy of the handout to read before small groups are formed. The content is also easily presented in PowerPoint or with overhead slides. Oral presentation of the information is a good option and allows questions to be asked. You can have someone on the reference team present the information or bring in an outside expert. It is important that whoever presents the staffing models avoids bringing in her personal bias. The decision really needs to be made by your library to fit your library's needs. Exercise 8-1 is designed to organize the discussion of staffing models and lead to a decision.

If your group is more than five people, divide into smaller groups of three to five. Try to compose groups of diverse staff (librarians and support staff, older and younger librarians, managers and frontline staff, etc.). If your staff is not too large, you can bring everyone into this exercise. If you have a large reference staff (twenty-five or more) you may need to use representatives, several sessions on staffing models, or otherwise adapt this exercise so as to not be too cumbersome.

The outcomes of exercise 8-1 are

➤ Revelation of people's preferences and concerns
➤ Sharing of ideas on locally workable models
➤ Discussion leading to convergence (and eventually a decision)

Follow the presentations with a short discussion of points of convergence and dissension. Remember, a decision on this issue does not need to be made today, but it does need to be made eventually. It may happen that the decision is made with this one-hour exercise, but do not be disappointed if the path is not this smooth. Designate someone to take notes of the presentations and outstanding discussion items to be returned to later.

NOTES

1. Anthony Ramirez, "Library Phone Answers Survive the Internet," *New York Times*, June 19, 2006, www.nytimes .com/2006/06/19/nyregion/19answer.html?pagewanted=1&ei=5070&en=0b9bbc01bf5db5f6&ex=1188964800.
2. Jana Smith Ronan, "Staffing a Real-Time Reference Service: The University of Florida Experience," *Internet Reference Services Quarterly* 8, nos. 1/2 (2003): 33–47.
3. Rick Roche, e-mail to M. K. Kern, March 1, 2007.
4. Matthew Bejune and Jane Kinkus, "Creating a Composite of User Behavior to Inform Decisions about New and Existing Library Services," *Reference Services Review* 34, no. 2 (2006): 185–192.

Small Group Decision on Staffing

One of your most important decisions during implementation will be how to staff the service. As a group, choose a model you think would work best for your service. Start by discussing internal staffing only, since you must make these decisions whether or not you are part of a consortium. Only if you have additional time should you discuss participation in a consortium.

Consider the following points in your discussion:

➤ What variations on the basic models are possible?

➤ Which of the staffing models (or variants) is most feasible for your library?

➤ Which staffing model will meet your goals for the service (refer to individual philosophies).

➤ What are the pros and cons of the model you have chosen? How might the negative aspects be mitigated?

➤ What will be your hours of operation for the pilot service? Would you want the same hours if the service becomes a permanent offering?

➤ If time permits, discuss participation in a consortium.

Prepare a three- to five-minute summary of your group's decision to present to the larger group.

CHAPTER 9

Assessing the Costs

BUDGETING FOR VIRTUAL REFERENCE

All services require money to operate. Most of the chapters in this book mention items that are part of the virtual reference budget, such as training, marketing, and staffing. Almost every decision you make has a budgetary implication. The previous chapters in this book offer ideas for minimizing costs and mention some of the trade-offs that may accompany a more leanly funded service. In this chapter I tie together the outcomes of your library's decisions with the appropriate area of budgeting. I also present a way to figure the cost of operating a virtual reference service. This method is a little different from the typical library budget, but the numbers you enter into the worksheet in this chapter can be plugged into a budget request and into line items in your library's budget.

The most important things I can say about budgeting are

- ➤ Plan from the start for the costs of a full service, funded from nongrant sources—even if you start with a limited pilot or on grant funding.
- ➤ Account for all costs, even if they are not part of a dedicated virtual reference budget.
- ➤ Consider the impacts on other units and consult with them about costs.
- ➤ Be realistic about budget needs, but also think creatively about ways to save money.
- ➤ It takes money to offer any worthwhile service—unless all of your library staff are volunteers and all of your materials are free. Even then, someone is paying.

Budget vs. Costing

The real cost of a virtual reference service is in most cases greater than the budget required to operate the service. This is because some costs are picked up by other departments and other costs are part of different funds and projects. Here's an example: If you have a marketing budget, costs of marketing and publicizing the new service to your patrons may be covered by that. A big marketing push may require a separate influx of funds, which may come from the virtual reference budget or from your library's regular marketing budget. Unless a library adds staff to start virtual reference, salaries are already paid as part of an existing salary budget line and are not part of a virtual reference budget.

The important thing in thinking about the cost of a virtual reference service is that, no matter where in the greater library budget the money comes from, it is still a cost of the service. I advise you to look at all costs of the service and then examine which are already paid for and which are part of a specific virtual reference budget.

Since I don't know anything about your library's fund structure, this chapter contains very little about budgets and a lot about costs.

Where Do the Costs Come From?

The costs associated with virtual reference are the same costs associated with any reference service, with the addition of the software/technical infrastructure and consortium fees, if applicable. The thing is, many libraries do not think about costs in terms of service. Budgets are usually set up around type of item rather than by service. Most libraries have no idea what the costs of operating circulation are. Could you answer the question "How much does reference cost?"

Worksheet 9-1 helps you determine the total cost of a virtual reference service. This worksheet is only an example and is likely not comprehensive of all the costs incurred by your library (e.g., indirect costs such as overhead and staff benefits are not included). It provides a high-level look at the service costs, which I think is sufficient; you can add more detail if that is your library's preference. Reference departments are reluctant to do this type of analysis lest they be singled out as having too high a cost. Nevertheless, it is important to know where your value is and to be able to support that assessment.

This worksheet may look alarming when completed. I assure you that performing the same activity for other services, such as a summer reading program, collection maintenance, or circulation, would produce similar results. Longer-term services have the advantage of being able to place costs next to outputs of their activities (number of children attending programs, books added to the collection, etc.). Once your library's virtual reference service has completed a cycle of activity (such as a budget year), it will have output data as well. Libraries and other nonprofits have the consideration of the less easily measured outputs such as impact on community economic development, increase in literacy, and student achievement. All the same, they are accountable for how the money is spent, and knowing the costs of a service as well as its outputs can aid in both budget justification and service planning.

IT Costing

The obvious technology cost is for the virtual reference software license itself. Paying for licensing of virtual reference software often includes support and hosting as part of the annual price. If you are part of a collaborative, the software is likely included in your annual membership fee. On the other hand, if you are hosting locally, costs related to servers and local staff must be considered even if they are part of the IT budget. How much staff time does your IT department predict will be spent on maintaining the software and servers involved with virtual reference? What is the average cost of the staff members to whom this work is assigned? If a server must be purchased, this is a one-time cost during the first year for the virtual reference service, even if IT agrees to pay for it

WORKSHEET 9-1 DETERMINING THE COSTS OF VIRTUAL REFERENCE SERVICE THROUGH YEAR 3

	NOTES	BUDGET LINE	YEAR 1 $	YEAR 2 $	YEAR 3 $
Software					
Yearly license/purchase		VR	Included in consortium fees		
Setup fee	One-time fee				
Hardware (for local hosting)	Consider replacement cycle for servers if hosting locally	Library IT	Need to ask IT	N/A	N/A
Technical support	Cost of library IT staff time if hosting locally	Library IT	Need to ask IT		
Marketing	Costs of design and production				
Assessment	Include costs for focus groups, surveys, etc.				
Training	Include travel, consulting, food, etc.				
Staff					
Permanent library staff to answer patron questions	Consider whether staff time is solely devoted to virtual reference questions for this calculation. Prorate as appropriate.	Existing salaries	0.10 FTE x 10 = ~60,000	Staffing from in-person desk, no increase in staffing needs for the library	
Permanent library staff involved in coordination of service	Percentage of permanent staff time devoted to assessment, marketing, management, etc. Prorate as appropriate.	New salary/VR	0.25 FTE = $15,000		
Vendor staff	Yearly cost for contract employees from software vendor	N/A	N/A	etc.	
Consortia fees/revenue	Cost of membership or credits if applicable	VR	$2,000	$2,000	$4,000
Other costs	This worksheet is not a comprehensive list.				
Total cost of service					

out of its budget. Find out if the server is dedicated to the virtual reference software or if other services are hosted in it. Upgrades and new equipment may be part of the regular IT workflow and not necessarily assigned to the virtual reference costing.

Costs for Staff

Librarians who staff the service a few hours a week as part of a job description that encompasses more than virtual reference are paid from a general salary line or from the salary lines of other units (depending on how your library distributes its budget funds). When there is a virtual reference coordinator whose entire time is dedicated to managing the service, this may be part of the virtual reference line item as well as part of the program costs. If you are part of a collaboration, some of the costs for administration are part of the annual fee you pay, but do not neglect to take into account staff time for meetings with the consortium and work such as assessment and scheduling that must be done locally even when part of a collaboration.

Planning for staff costs over a three-year period brings in some special considerations. During the first year, there will be additional staff time required for training and for planning. Staff costs increase over time because of raises and increasing costs of benefits. Your human resources department should be able to supply an average rate for the annual increase.

Marketing

If you hire a designer or a marketing consultant, then that is an obvious cost. Advertisements, flyers, and giveaways are other costs related to the marketing of virtual reference. Your library may have a designer or a marketing team. If you are this lucky, be sure to account for the time that they spend specifically on virtual reference. Marketing costs may vary greatly from year to year, and so a marketing plan will be useful in your predicting costs.

Start-up vs. Recurring Costs

Some costs are incurred only once, at the beginning of the service. This may seem obvious, but it can be easily overlooked if the focus is on the "standard" virtual reference budget, so careful consideration should be given to this category. What new equipment will be purchased? This might be as extra or upgraded workstations, speakers or headsets, or a desk. Equipment may become part of a regular pool that is replaced on a cycle, but when something new or out of the ordinary is requested, it is not normal operating overhead. The costs incurred from the planning process need to be included and are certainly much higher in the first year. The costs of planning may include meetings, training, incentives (for focus group participants), and any outside consulting. Important to note is that meetings and training are mainly increases related to the costs of staff. For clarity, the staff costs of meetings and training should be distinct on the costing worksheet so that they are not confused with the costs of staffing the service to answer questions.

A major advantage to doing the costing exercise for three years is that it helps determine where in the budget costs will be borne. If administration (or a grant) is providing for start-up costs, where is the money in the budget for subsequent years? Does this become part of the line items that already exist, or will there be a separate line for virtual reference—and what is it expected to encompass? If there are costs being absorbed into the budgets of other units, such as marketing or IT, it is critical that these units are aware of this from the start and that they know the predicted costs. A commitment to providing for the projected needs of the virtual reference service is important for sustained success.

Who Pays?

The total cost to the library of operating a virtual reference service includes items that may come from budget lines outside the part of the budget devoted to virtual reference. This would likely include costs of staff time spent answering questions and library IT staff time spent in technical support. Depending on how the library arranges its budget, marketing costs may be paid from a general budget for public relations, and assessment of the service may be part of a larger budget for assessment. It is important to determine not only what money is needed but from where in the library's budget it will come. Worksheet 9-1 includes a column for designating the budget line where the cost occurs.

After completing the costing exercise, you will be able to see clearly which items are to be paid for from a specially designated virtual reference budget. From this you can develop the budget for this service. There may be some areas where the costs are paid from another budget, but the virtual reference budget may need to pay occasionally for special projects or one-time capital expenses.

Make a Long-Term Plan

The costing worksheet covers three years. Even if your service starts as a pilot, budgeting should be planned for several years. If the service does not continue beyond the pilot phase, then that budget will not be needed. An important part of moving a service from a pilot into a permanent service is having a budget in place to facilitate the transition. This can cause a bump, particularly when the pilot has been limited and done "on the cheap" in a way that will not support a service with longer hours, more training, and a marketing campaign. Failure to plan for a continuing service reflects a lack of faith in success.

Fewer virtual reference services start with grant funding today than in 2000–2004. Although grants for start-up may still be available, they are rarely available for established services. Sustainability of a grant-funded project into the post-grant phase relies on identification of a source of funding, and a budget is a necessary part of this planning. A budget the library can sustain should be determined at the inception of the service. If the service is not continued after the grant, it will not be due to lack of ability to fund the project (unless there is a major change in the budget for you library). If the budget is not used for virtual reference, it can always be used elsewhere—but better to have earmarked the money from the start than to struggle at the end of the grant.

For some librarians, part of the appeal of pilots and grants is that they provide the library with a low-cost or funded test phase, and this is translated into limited commitment. It is certainly acceptable after the test phase to discontinue a service if the assessments support this decision. The commitment to continue should, however, be present from the start.

CHAPTER 10

Collaborative Virtual Reference

Collaborative virtual reference projects started almost simultaneously with virtual reference in libraries. Although libraries do not have a rich history of cooperation in the area of providing reference services, we do have a history of cooperating in other areas such as interlibrary loan and shared licensing of electronic resources. The nature of virtual reference as not place-bound opened up the possibilities for collaboration, and libraries applied their old urge to cooperate to the new cyberworld. There are many different models of collaborative virtual reference, but at essence it is an arrangement between two or more libraries to offer virtual reference services to each other's patrons.

The Library of Congress was one of the early movers in collaborative virtual reference. The Collaborative Digital Reference Service (CDRS) operated in the early 2000s as an e-mail-only collaboration. The CDRS initiative became one of the foundations for QuestionPoint as the Library of Congress partnered with OCLC, and now chat is part of the service offering. Two statewide collaborations in particular—QandA NJ and Maryland AskUsNow!—have been mainstays in the virtual reference scene for many years. Other collaborations such as that between the University of Washington and Cornell University have been tried and terminated. As with any type of virtual reference, collaborative arrangements have to prove their benefit to the library and to its patrons. An added burden on a collaborative virtual reference service is that it has to prove its worth to every member library or libraries will leave the collaboration, shrinking the size of the group and possibly the benefits.

The decision to be made is whether collaboration is right for your library. There are other considerations that must be made on the consortium level, and a few of those are covered here. If you are starting a consortium rather than joining an existing one, the VR Guidelines offer more detail, as do the Guidelines for Cooperative Reference Services.[1]

Benefits of Collaboration

As demonstrated by more than thirty statewide consortia, several national collaborations (such as are present in Norway and Australia), as well as smaller collaborations among a few libraries, there are benefits to joining together to offer virtual reference as a group.[2] OCLC's QuestionPoint even expands the collaboration options to an international group of libraries with more than two thousand member libraries worldwide.

Shared Staffing

The most often mentioned and most obvious reason for joining a collaboration is to share the hours of staffing with other libraries. Staff is the largest cost in operating a service, even if a library hires no new staff to do so. Members of a consortium can opt to lower their individual library's staff commitment to a few hours a week and still provide their patrons with extended hours of service, sometimes even 24/7.

Sharing staff does not necessarily lower a library's commitment, for some libraries choose to offer virtual reference through their own service during normal hours of operation and also staff a few consortium hours in order to participate in the 24/7 or after-hours option. This decision is based primarily on a library's wish to assist its local patrons as much as possible and use the consortium only for additional support.

Shared Money Goes Farther

Together, libraries can use their collective money to achieve what is not possible for a single library. Libraries do this frequently for licensing of databases and other collections, but it is true in the area of services as well. Libraries that are part of strong statewide or regional cooperatives already realize this, but it may be a new idea for others.

Training and marketing are the two biggest areas where shared money makes an impact. With pooled resources (and grant money) Washington State Library was able to provide professional marketing materials to its member libraries, including clever radio advertisements. Maryland AskUsNow! chose to market the statewide service to establish a single point of contact and name recognition for the service. This type of statewide campaign benefited all of the libraries involved but required more resources than any single library would have been willing to fund.

Training benefits come from sharing materials, developing online tutorials, and hiring training experts to lead sessions. Training experts and online tutorials may cost more in money or time than most libraries can afford on their own. When retraining is necessary to maintain quality, this may be better received from an employee of the consortium than from a colleague at the same library. American University and George Washington University continued this part of their collaboration even after ceasing to offer a shared, collaborative virtual reference service.

Consortia also often have better grant-writing and grant-receiving capabilities. Funding agencies have high regard for proven collaborations and the efficiencies they can bring to a project. They also hope, rightly or wrongly, that a consortium will ensure the continuation of a project beyond the grant phase.

Assessment and Administrative Resources

Undertaking an in-depth assessment of a virtual reference service takes time and expertise. Chapter 13 covers ways to make assessment a manageable and still meaningful task for a single library. Collaborations may be able to call on an assessment expert from a member library or on the consortium staff to conduct a comprehensive assessment plan. Grant-funded projects may have monies for an outside assessment team included and a requirement for completion of the grant.

Expanded Expertise and Resources

Assessment is not the only area in which shared expertise is an advantage. Libraries and librarians have their own expertise. An academic library may be able to provide experts in technical and academic subjects. Other librarians may be able to provide local history, genealogy assistance, or homework help. All librarians have their own areas of interest and skill, such as foreign languages or knowledge from past careers. Children's librarians can offer recommendations about age-appropriate literature. Multitype collaborations may include special libraries such as medical or government documents repositories, which can assist patrons with areas of inquiry not handled by other members of the consortium.

Collaborative reference also opens up the collections of many libraries for use in answering questions, making everyone's collection useful to a broader audience. Thus, collaboration expands the base of knowledge available to the patron.

Making the Impossible Possible

Without collaboration, many libraries would not find virtual reference a viable service. This is especially true of smaller libraries with a handful of staff and limited building hours. The Antioch (pop. 8,700) and Newton (pop. 3,000) public libraries are part of the AskAway Illinois collaborative. Joining a collaboration can increase a library's value to its community by extending the hours of available reference service and enabling the addition of virtual reference without expanding local staffing.

Issues in Collaboration

Just as there are many benefits that draw libraries to collaborative virtual reference, there are also problem areas that keep libraries from joining or cause them to leave.

Maintaining Quality

Libraries worry about the quality of service and accuracy of answers provided to their patrons from consortia. Even within our own libraries, various studies have called to our attention that as a profession we can improve in these areas. Consortia bring with them an added level of complexity, which may impact service quality. The range of questions may be broader than individual librarians are used to fielding, and this can cause a strain on both these librarians and their patrons; public libraries find academic questions difficult to handle, and academic libraries have little idea what to do with a junior high school student.

What a librarian may know to be just a question of pushing her comfort zone can be viewed by a patron as incompetence. Some of the quality issues can be managed through good reference interviews and developing rapport in online communication. Librarians are faced with questions in subjects entirely new to them even when they are staffing at their own libraries. This situation may become more frequent in a collaboration, and if there is no recourse to forwarding the question to another librarian, tension rises, especially with chat questions.

Local Questions and Patrons

Librarians feel, often with justification, that we know our local populations better than other librarians or vendors do. This is why we resist outsourcing of collection development and cataloging. Collaborative virtual reference can feel somewhat like outsourcing of our reference questions, especially when a library feels that it has less contact with its local patrons than before joining the consortium. This is why some libraries opt to maintain a local question queue within the consortium. Local patrons can be directed to a local librarian when one is available. If it is feasible for the library to staff this way, it is a definite benefit to the patron.

When it comes to questions with clear right and wrong answers (such as local library policies), the issues of quality become most apparent. Consortia often develop staff web pages to assist librarians with answering local questions, but many questions must be referred back to the local library since nonlocal librarians are typically unable to interpret policies or questions about local resources.

Libraries with clientele in specialized subject areas not handled by other libraries in the consortium may also feel at a disadvantage. For example, if an academic library serves a large off-campus nursing program, and no other library in the consortium serves nursing students, then training may be required to bring other librarians up to a basic level of service in this subject. Quality and "localness" can, to a limited extent, be addressed through training. Some patrons are always happy to receive any response and do not care where the librarian is located; others may be dismayed if the nonlocal librarian is not able to answer the question fully or needs to refer them back to the home library. When assessing the success of a collaborative service, be sure to review individual transcripts to determine how well questions of a "local" nature (library policies, circulation, community information, etc.) are answered.

For the story of one library that left a collaboration to offer assistance to its own patrons through IM, read the Library Field Report "Closing a Consortium, Moving to IM, Trying VoIP."

Databases and Resources

Even when librarians are ready to answer all questions from all libraries and all users, there can be barriers in the online environment. The databases owned by one library may not be available to another. This makes helping a patron who needs a specific online resource difficult. If, for example, a patron from Big State U has a question best answered by Pollution Abstracts, but Big State U is the only member of the consortium that has access to that resource and I am at Big City Public, the best I can do is direct the patron to this resource and perhaps suggest search terms. I cannot assist much with the search since I cannot see the results to help refine the search terms or evaluate the

Closing a Consortium, Moving to IM, Trying VoIP

At the end of the 2005/6 academic year, American University and its Washington Research Library Consortium (WRLC) partners closed their private, academic QuestionPoint collaborative network. American University librarian Alex Hodges said that, after four or five years of "hard work using several chat software programs," the WRLC decided to abandon chat. "It was a really painful experience for everyone."

"We felt we would have more local control if we had our own IM service, and we wanted to be where our users were." Instant Messaging software does not support a collaborative environment.

"The consortial service had more than seventy librarians, all of whom had an MLS. At American, we don't have seventy librarians. We only have twenty librarian faculty members."

"A huge component of gaining staff for our IM reference service has been to recruit people from outside the reference faculty to help provide the service," said Hodges. This includes extending staffing to nonlibrarian staff members who have an interest in reference service, some of whom are pursuing their MLS degrees.

In this way, the American University library can come up with the people necessary to run the service while providing interested staff members an opportunity to gain experience—what Hodges calls "a training program for nonlibrarians."

The former WRLC partners continue to share best practices through a Google group, http://groups.google.com/group/lmbestpractices.

As part of expanding services to its local users, American University has started a VoIP service, which is still at an early stage. Hodges says that so far most of the library's VoIP interactions have begun with IM sessions that have transferred to VoIP at the suggestion of the librarian. (And several attempts at VoIP conversations have ended up being conducted over the phone instead. Hodges says he sometimes gives patrons his office telephone number as well, when attempting to initiate VoIP.) Hodges has had one user initiate a VoIP communication.

Hodges does voice concern over patron privacy as related to VoIP and the CALEA Act. But, he says, "A lot of us librarians like the option that it's there."

"The bottom line is that we still need to be talking about virtual reference and adapting our services in the best way possible for our users."

Alex Hodges, Instruction Coordinator/Reference Librarian, American University

Interview by Lena Singer

results. This is just a reality of database licensing. Sometimes, getting the patron pointed in the right direction with the suggestion to contact a specific library or librarian is appreciated—more than the librarian might expect, given the limitations.

Communication and Training

The larger the organization, the more communication it requires. Communication is fundamental to continuous training as well as to making people feel included and involved.

There are many easy communication and collaboration tools, beyond e-mail, to provide training and announcements. Wikis and blogs, which are discussed in chapter 14, are ways for librarians to communicate as a group as well as for consortium administrators to disseminate information to librarians. All of this communicating does take time to generate and to read. There should also be guidelines about what information should be shared broadly and what may be issues to bring to an administrator.

Training for specialized and local questions is an additional obligation for training in collaborative virtual reference. With the added question types, training may need to be more frequent.

Trust

Collaborations cannot work without trust. Forming a consortium does not automatically create trust. Even when a consortium exists prior to offering collaborative virtual reference, trust may not be present. Trust is what is ultimately behind the question "Do I want you to answer my patrons' questions?"

Communication, including acknowledging that trust can be tricky, is important to building rapport within the collaborative. Feeling that your colleagues are adequately trained and ready to assist your patron is also important. Some consortia have even established testing for competencies to help with the issues of quality and trust. Review of interactions by administrators can also help with trust by catching problem areas with the service and addressing them with individual librarians and libraries before they take on consortium-wide proportions.

Finding a Collaboration

Existing Consortia

Virtual reference consortia sometimes form around existing library cooperation. Libraries that pool resources for electronic databases or shared training programs already have a base from which to build and administer a virtual reference working relationship. These may be organized around type of library, such as medical libraries or four-year college libraries. Or they may have a geographic component, such as the Michigan Community Colleges' Research Help Now, the Boston Library Consortium, and the OhioLINK academic libraries collaboration.[3]

Statewide

There are quite a few statewide consortia, and they are easy to find through a web search. Some are projects of the state library and others are independent groups. There are also regional collaboratives that often are organized around existing regional administrative groups. As mentioned earlier, a few countries have national services. The major virtual reference vendors can provide you with a list of cooperative services that use their software.

Library to Library

Some libraries choose to be selective and form partnerships with one or two other libraries that they handpick to meet certain requirements: "Seeking a liberal arts college interested in forming a virtual reference collaboration. Must be in the Eastern or Pacific time zone." Libraries don't have to place ads though, because we know the profiles of other libraries quite well and can make contacts without the blind-date approach.

These smaller collaborations usually do not extend hours as far as larger partnerships. Other benefits can be gained from similarity of user population, complementary subjects (either because of overlap or providing expertise that the other library lacks), or differences in hours of operation.

Multiple Configurations

In addition, a library can belong to more than one group, and some consortia are nested, as with a regional collaboration being part of a statewide group. A library may be part of a statewide public library group that is in turn part of a statewide multitype group or national public library group. Don't be overwhelmed. Start by identifying a consortium or two and talk with them about their structures and options before making a decision.

Internal Collaborations

Some libraries and library systems are dispersed enough to require their own internal collaborative arrangements. At the University of Florida, librarians from eight different departments staff the RefeXpress service. In a 2002 article, Jana Ronan explained that each UF librarian staffed two hours a week, and issues of scheduling and coordination were handled by one librarian designated to manage the project. In a later article she noted that there can be issues related to assessment when librarians are coordinated by someone who is not their supervisor and may, in fact, be their junior.[4] The arrangement at the UF libraries allowed them to expand the hours for the virtual reference service and to provide the expertise of their subject librarians to virtual users.

At my library, we have a sort of internal collaboration across our several subject libraries. This draws on our academic experts and makes them more visible to students and researchers, who increasingly work from outside the library. Some of the subject libraries also answer questions that may "overflow" when the central service is busy. The collaboration also takes advantage of the different traffic patterns at the main and undergraduate libraries, since we can pick up questions from each other's queues. As our IM questions have increased and our chat questions have declined, it has become more challenging to realize the workflow benefits of the collaboration. We are hopeful that a collaborative IM product will appear.

Unique Considerations

My Queue or Yours

The existence of multiple-question queues and shared-question queues is unique to collaborative virtual reference. Many permutations are possible; if you can imagine it, it can probably be set up in the software. Work with a consortium administrator to determine options and find the one that best fits your library's needs. This decision can likely be changed later if a different staffing and queuing option becomes more appropriate.

Most libraries like to think that they are reaching some of their own patrons. When this does not happen, libraries are more likely to seek other reference options. Rick Roche at Thomas Ford Memorial Library shares the reasons his library is likely to not renew membership in the statewide consortium:

> We didn't have to pay much to join, and I don't think there's really much consequence to us. But, I don't see that our patron base is using it. Our local people are more likely to contact us by IM. I don't think it will hamper the state effort—they've only given us a one-hour assignment. I don't think we'll be missed. Some places are enjoying it, and some are using it a lot more. It's just not the direction we're going.[5]

Consortia should talk with exiting libraries to determine ways they can improve on all levels, with particular attention paid to effective queuing and staffing models.

Policy Agreement

The consortium will have a set of policies for the collaboration itself, apart from whatever local policies the members might have. In addition, there may be policies, such as parameters of service, that all members of the consortium are asked to follow. If your library is a founding member of a consortium, you will most likely be involved in the creation of these policies. When joining an existing consortium, a new library may not have much opportunity to change the policies already in place.

As with other types of library consortia, organization and administration of the group vary. There may be a governing board or a single coordinator. There may be user group meetings at which policies and other issues are discussed, and there may be other ways for members to influence decision making. It is worthwhile to find out about the mechanism for member contribution to issues of policy. When signing on to a collaboration, it is also important to consider whether its policies fit those of your own library; if changes are needed locally, your library must decide who will vet the new policies.

The Guidelines for Cooperative Reference Service, mentioned earlier, offer some guidance on consortial policies. Many virtual reference collaborations are forthcoming with their internal documentation, so if you are forming a new collaborative (or revising documentation for an existing one) ask some other collaborations for their policies and administrative documents.

Coordination Equals Administration

Steering a group requires coordination. Even when there is not a full-time administrator, one or more people must take care of the finances, the scheduling, the policies, arrangements for training, and the like. This may come in the form of a dedicated manager or a management team. Duties may also be distributed to different libraries, with one library coordinating training and another scheduling, for instance. The later arrangement seems to require more trust and communication among member libraries, since it is essentially a volunteer arrangement. This is an arrangement that seems to me to be noble but untenable.

Pricing and Contribution Models

Unless each member of the consortium pays for its own software and the administration is entirely contributed by the member libraries, there will be membership fees. Group pricing and administration of the vendor contract are frequently benefits of being part of a collaborative virtual reference group, so expect to pay something to be a member and expect benefits in return. Pricing for a member library may be based on size of library population, number of questions users asked in the previous year, number of hours the library can contribute to the service, or a flat fee.

Contribution of staffing hours for the collaboration varies along similar lines: more hours may be required of larger libraries. Libraries may also be able to pay more and staff fewer hours. Libraries providing staff to manage the service may request a reduction in the amount of money they contribute or the number of hours they staff the service. By way of example, AskColorado has "suggested" contributions posted on their website at www.aclin.org/reference/join.html.

Equitability

As mentioned at the start of the chapter, there must be benefit for all members of the collaboration for it to be successful. No library should feel that it is carrying more of the service than it receives benefit for doing. It may be the case that some larger libraries contribute more in money or more in hours and may answer questions from many nonlocal patrons. These libraries my feel that they are contributing to something positive and that their portion does not constitute a burden. Still, they and all libraries must feel that membership benefits them and their patrons.

NOTES

1. "Guidelines for Cooperative Reference Services," Reference and User Services Association, June 2006, www.ala.org/ala/rusa/protools/referenceguide/guidelinescooperative.cfm.
2. A list of province-wide and statewide virtual reference collaborations is maintained by the Alberta AskAQuestion service: http://askaquestion.ab.ca/referral.html.
3. Note that these groups were active as I was writing this chapter, but names, participants, and even their existence may have changed by now.
4. Jana Ronan, "Staffing a Real-Time Reference Service: The University of Florida Experience," *Internet Reference Services Quarterly* 8, nos. 1/2 (2003): 33–47. Jana Ronan, Patrick Reakes, and Gary Cornwell, "Evaluating Online Real-Time Reference in an Academic Library: Obstacles and Recommendations," *Reference Librarian* 38 nos. 79/80 (2003): 225–240.
5. Rick Roche, e-mail message to M. K. Kern, March 1, 2007.

CHAPTER 11

Aspects of Training

Training for virtual reference is essential to a successful service. Continuous learning and development of skills should be encouraged, as should the environment and tools to allow this to happen. Initial training prior to the service is not an extensive process. The best teachers here are experience and practice.

Software

Several years ago, virtual reference vendors used to send trainers to libraries to provide training in their software. This was promoted as a necessary service, not just one to use if you had a small staff or no one willing to lead training, because the software was complicated and the concepts new. I always thought that if the software was that difficult for the librarian to use it should be redesigned. The reference aspect was already familiar to librarians, and we are generally adept at learning new interfaces and programs. There are good reasons to bring in an outside trainer, but difficulty of the software should not be one of them. Fortunately, virtual reference software keeps getting easier to use, and the longer it has been in use, the more familiar it seems to libraries, even those new to the service.

Group Training

The most efficient way to train on anything is to assemble a group: one trainer, many trainees. This is also an effective way to train on virtual reference software, but do not let the class size get out of hand. Twelve people are about all one trainer can handle without an assistant. Some of this has to do with the existing skills and comfort levels of the staff being trained, but I find this to be a good rule of thumb.

When I do training for virtual reference (which I do every year for our new graduate assistants), I start with a demonstration of an online conversation. I set up a partner to ask me a predetermined question, and then I provide a live, but short, example of a virtual reference interaction. I start with this so that I know everyone in the room will have a visual idea of online communication. Next, I cover policies and communications to provide context for the software training.

In my overview of the software features, I emphasize why they might be used—not just where the canned messages are located, but what function they serve and when to use them. I try to leave about half of the training time for hands-on practice with the software. I divide the group into pairs. One person takes the role of the librarian and the other of the patron (see exercise 11-1). Once I see that people are getting used to the software, I flip the roles. I try to assign the librarian role first to those with more experience with online communication. This is easy if I know the participants. Otherwise I ask early on in the training for a show of hands: who has used virtual reference software or IM before?

Providing some time for trainees to just communicate in the software is nice if time permits. This can get them comfortable with the software without the pressure of the reference interview. Still, the reference interview online is substantially different from casual conversation, so I've learned to provide a more structured exercise that provides the pairs with real-life reference questions. Walking around the room to observe the librarians' reference interviews and to answer questions about the software or the communication allows me to give more personalized assistance and informs me about what follow-up training might be required.

When the group software training is finished, I leave the librarians with the log-ins for the training accounts and encourage them to find a time to practice with a buddy. Training takes one and a half to two hours, depending on the previous experience of the librarians and how many people are being trained. More time should be allotted for training that also covers policies. If more than two hours is needed, consider dividing the content into software and nonsoftware training, with a break in between. If the staff feel uncertain with the software, schedule a less formal "group practice" after the training where the trainer can be present to assist, answer questions, and reassure.

Internal Use of IM

A great hands-on way to learn the software is to use it for internal communications. This is most easily done with IM where everyone has their own account. Registering individual accounts can take place during group training, but it may be easier to handle one-on-one with the librarians. Some librarians will likely already have accounts, and some will accomplish the set-up without assistance. The registration is probably the most difficult part about using IM, since the rest is basically typing. If IM is new but the library has used chat software, the training required should be minimal. The same can be said for embedded chat. A librarian at my library observed me using our Meebo interface and said, "If you already know IM, there is really nothing to learn, is there?"—which is exactly what a trainer wants to hear.

Once accounts are established, the librarians can practice using it in place of the telephone to ask questions and to invite each other to coffee. This develops casual familiarity with the software, which carries over into the more formal reference interaction. It also gives the librarian an idea of how patrons use IM in their daily lives.

Practice with Chat/IM Communication

Work in pairs, designating one person as the "librarian" and one person as the "patron." Give the patron Question set 1.

The designated librarian logs into the librarian interface. The designated patron uses either his IM account or the patron interface to the library's virtual reference service.

Using the question set, practice asking and answering questions. After ten to fifteen minutes, switch roles and have the new patron use Question set 2.

This is a chance to practice using the interface but also to experience conducting an online reference interview and navigating patrons through the research process. The parts of the question in parentheses are clarifying information. The patron should wait for a prompting question from the librarian before providing this amount of detail about the question, to best simulate the process of a real reference encounter.

PRACTICE QUESTIONS, SET 1

1. How long can I check out a book?

2. Is the library open this weekend?

3. Does the library own Cat in the Hat?

4. Where do I go to vote?

5. I need articles on drugs and athletes. (college athletes, illegal drugs)

6. The librarian showed my class how to find information about businesses, but I can't remember how. Can you help me?

7. Hi. Can you help me find articles on gun control? I need to say how it is a good thing.

PRACTICE QUESTIONS, SET 2

1. What does "on reserve" mean for a book?

2. When is the next community theater production?

3. Does the library own Everything Is Miscelaneous?

4. How do I get a book from another library?

5. I need articles for my paper on Hispanics and voting. (in presidential elections)

6. Hi, are you a real person? (wait for reply from librarian) Can you help me find articles on the impact of No Child Left Behind?

Communication

Training on best practices in online communications is essential even for the most experienced and adept reference librarian. There are some differences in online communication that need to be explained and practiced. Providing some examples of bad, good, and better online conversation is a humorous and pointed way to teach this. See figure 11-1 for an example. Keep the examples to ones that are obviously made up and not from real life to avoid the tension that might be created by more realistic examples. As this example shows, different responses can each be accurate and appropriate but still represent varying levels of quality of communication. This lets people see that there is not a single right way to communicate, that some tactics work better than others. Emphasize that, just as every librarian has his own in-person style of communicating with patrons, each librarian has his own online style. Individual style makes us more human to the patron, and variation is desirable as long as it falls within the best practices covered in chapter 7.

Policies

If you have designed your library's virtual reference policies as a group, this training may be short. It should still be covered to make sure there has not been any drift in thinking, that everyone is on the same page.

If policies have been set by the administration or your group is otherwise unfamiliar with them, allow enough time to communicate the relevant policy areas and answer a lot of questions. Policy should always be accompanied by the underlying philosophy and how it is practiced at your library.

FIGURE 11-1 SETTING THE TONE IN VIRTUAL COMMUNICATIONS

Lostinthestacks: I am so dumb

Lostinthestacks: Where do I find the books?

Lostinthestacks: can you help me?

Consider the above patron inquiry, and the following possible responses:

Librarian 1: You will need to go to the main stacks.

Librarian 2: Can you tell me the book that you need?

Librarian 3: Our library is big and can be confusing. What book do you need?

Which librarian's response is better? Why?

Which do you feel most comfortable with? How would you respond in your own words to Lostinthestacks?

Ongoing Training and Review

Communicating Training Materials

As a matter of course, everyone should be provided with training materials during the group training. If materials are not printed, it should be clear where they can be obtained on the library website or internal file server. Training updates will be necessary. New best practices may be realized, policies may change, or everyone may need to learn about the paper that was just assigned to a class of three hundred local students.

Blogs are useful for news-flash items like the just-mentioned class assignment and for directing staff to new training documents. E-mail is good as well, except that messages get deleted or lost in the in-box. Wikis are a better option for posting documents and information that have more enduring value, such as how to troubleshoot remote access to your online databases. Websites are quite acceptable for this type of documentation as well, although they lack the participatory aspect that allows librarians to share their own tips on how to help patrons when the library catalog is unexpectedly offline.

Quality Assurance

Some libraries review transcripts from their virtual reference transactions for issues of accuracy and tone—in short, for quality. This type of transcript review can be a sticky issue. Many librarians are not used to having their reference interactions evaluated. It may seem intrusive and scary. If your library can designate a librarian to review transcripts for accuracy and tone, this can help with quality online and through other modes of communication. For example, every year I find that at least one person on the staff has forgotten the criteria for when to send patrons to interlibrary lending. If I catch this early enough, I can prevent misinformation from spreading to the entire reference staff. Correction is often most comfortably approached as training or reminders to the group. This is particularly the case when the virtual reference manager is not the supervisor of the staffing librarians. If there are significant quality or communication issues with a single staff member, it can be dealt with individually with tact and amended with training.

Self-Evaluation

Guided self-evaluation can be effective and less confrontational than review provided by a colleague. To make this type of evaluation effective, the librarians should be provided with a method and desired outcomes. Each librarian can be asked to review her own transcripts or to look at transcripts from other libraries or old transcripts if either can be obtained. Librarian anonymity can be provided by removing names, dates, and times from the transcript, but in a small library individuals may still be recognized by their style. The point is to not have librarians evaluating one another.

David Ward, from the University of Illinois at Urbana, developed an exercise for evaluation of the reference interview process. Librarians first review old transcripts using a list of criteria and later perform a self-evaluation. The emphases are on online communication as a process and self-improvement through discovery of best-practices. The Research You Can Use in this chapter provides detail about Ward's methodology and the outcomes from the self-assessment process.

Using Virtual Reference Transcripts for Staff Training

David Ward, Undergraduate Library Reference Coordinator, University of Illinois, Urbana-Champaign, *Reference Services Review* 31, no. 1 (2003): 46–56.

One of virtual reference's defining advantages is the transcript—an invaluable tool for evaluation built directly into the interaction. David Ward's study shows that you can transfer this evaluation aspect to training, creating an opportunity to encourage critical thinking and self-reflection among staff about how successful reference interviews are conducted online.

Librarians have commonly used transcripts to monitor the quality of virtual reference interactions. In 2003, Ward employed chat transcripts as training tools for graduate student workers, with encouraging results.

Eleven graduate student workers from the university's undergraduate library reference desk were asked to examine the transcripts of chat reference interactions that had taken place in libraries across campus. The students were then asked to answer questions about the interactions based on RUSA's standards for reference interviews.

The study had three main objectives: to raise student workers' awareness of the profession's standards for reference interviews, to educate them about the interview process, and to encourage critical thinking about how the individual components of the reference interview converge to deliver a successful reference interaction.

It is important to keep in mind that student workers were not asked to evaluate the quality of the interviews per se. They were never prompted to comment on whether they thought, based on a transcript, that an interview had been good or bad. As Ward wrote, a "rating or ranking mindset" was avoided.

Instead, students were encouraged to "consider the process as one of identifying and recognizing the important parts of a reference interview and their impacts." They were asked to determine whether a librarian had displayed virtual "approachability" (through "emoticons," for example, or casual language adapted to the patron's) or interest in an online patron's question; asked open- or closed-ended questions or paraphrased the patron's query; walked the patron through the steps of the online search; and closed the interview with follow-up questions, encouraged the patron to visit the library in person, or both.

After the study, the student workers performed self-evaluations. According to Ward, "of the 12 skills which each student rated, 11 showed improvement by at least one member of the group at the end." (The twelfth skill was indicated as having been understood fully by everyone before and after the study.) Although there were areas about which students indicated they felt less confident than before they had examined the transcripts, they admitted that these feelings stemmed from the fact that they did not know as much about those steps of the reference interview as they thought they did.

In the end, the study provided students with the advantage of becoming "experts" in reference interview standards and procedures while being able to identify, based on what they learned, the areas in which they could improve. And the library was able to raise the level of service provided in a key service point by educating paraprofessional staff in the best practices of virtual reference.

Any library can perform this type of transcript evaluation as a part of staff training. The twelve points Ward used are listed in his article.

Summary by Lena Singer

Training for the Administrator

Virtual reference service managers need training too. Vendors often provide online tutorials for software administrators. Consortia may provide training in the administrative interface and "train the trainer" sessions to provide local service managers with the resources to train their own staff. Buff Hirko's book *Virtual Reference Training* contains numerous exercises to use in training and tools to develop your own training curriculum.[1] The material was developed from the Washington State Library's virtual reference training program and can be used regardless of your library's virtual reference software.

Many of us teach ourselves the software and explore new software options by reading mailing lists, tech blogs, and articles. As a manager or software administrator, it can be easy to forget to document what you know. Take time to do this, noting changes as they happen. Record local customizations that are different from the software default so that you can quickly make the changes again if they are lost in a software upgrade or through your own error. Consider your successor; you may leave and the next service manager would love to know the passwords to all your virtual reference accounts. Quirks of the software that you know about are better not rediscovered by someone new, and configurations should not be a guessing game. Documentation is also an aid to your own memory because, when systems run well and need little attention, details like passwords and configurations can be forgotten.

NOTE

1. Buff Hirko, *Virtual Reference Training: The Complete Guide to Providing Anytime, Anywhere Answers* (Chicago: American Library Association, 2004).

CHAPTER 12

Marketing Your Virtual Reference Service

Promotion of virtual reference service is essential, but marketing is often something librarians do not feel they do well. Your new virtual reference service is likely to see little use if no one knows about it and it is buried too deeply on the library's website for users to find. The challenge is to build awareness of the service in terms of both brand recognition and functionality.

We reviewed finding your target market in chapter 3. A full marketing plan can be extensive (and a good idea); for that I refer you to Fisher and Pride's *Blueprint for Your Library Marketing Plan*.[1] In this chapter I address some of the fundamentals of marketing specific to virtual reference and offer some ideas and tips for making marketing less expensive and easier for the amateur.

Simple Ideas

Giveaways

Things, physical items, given to patrons to advertise your service are easy, and there are plenty of companies that sell a variety of promotional items. Some giveaways you can produce within your own library. And I am not talking about bookmarks; I am not sure how much sense bookmarks make for a virtual service. Some examples of giveaways include the following:

> The University of North Carolina at Chapel Hill used the easy and clever idea of "Hello My Name Is . . ." stickers to promote its IM buddy (or screen) name. The stickers can be bought at any office supply store. Other stickers can be made using your library's printer and sticker-backed paper. Look at craft and office supply stores for paper precut on one side to fun shapes.

> Maryland AskUsNow! distributed key chains with highlighter attached. I kept that one until it ran out because it was useful and always at hand.

> Flickr cards are fun and not terribly expensive. It is amazing how a fragment of a photo can look so much better than the full photo. There is just enough room on the back for your URL, IM screen name, and a tagline.

FIGURE 12-1   "CONFUSED? ASK A LIBRARIAN!" ERIK KRAFT (DESIGNER)

Reproduced with the permission of the University Library, University of Illinois at Urbana.

Business cards are not exactly a fun giveaway, but they can be made to look edgy or more formal. You can see two versions of my library's Ask a Librarian business card in figure 12-1. The more formal one is used to give out to faculty, and the edgier one was distributed at our desk.

Consider the longevity and usefulness of a giveaway: a plastic ID holder that is used daily reinforces awareness of your service; a highlighter is used at times when a student is studying and might be a reminder at point of need; magnets are durable and visible. Present some options that are within your price range to readily available members of your target audiences to obtain instant feedback. You don't need to look far for people to help with selection of promotional items—library volunteers, family members, student employees all can be sources of good ideas. Reaching beyond the library's immediate sphere is good; obtain samples from companies that sell promotional items and give them to friends, family, friends of friends, and co-workers of family (keeping in mind that the recipients are part of the target group) and ask for a reaction. These sample items are going to be overstock from other businesses' campaigns, so you won't get feedback on the message but rather on the item itself. Key things to ask: Is it appealing to them? Will they keep it and use it again? When would they see themselves using the item?

Prominent Placement of Link

The issue with giveaways is that they still require the patron to be physically present at some point to pick up the item. They can be distributed outside of library, but you still may be missing the hoards of patrons who use your library electronically and may not frequent the events where you hand out the freebies.

Placement of a link to your service in a prominent place on your website is the single best (and least expensive) way to promote your virtual reference service. QandA NJ surveyed its virtual reference patrons and found out how they learned about their service:[2]

35%	Link on library web page
27%	Word of mouth (friends, family, teacher)
13%	Article in newspaper or magazine

13%	Search engine
9%	Posters/bookmarks
7%	Link on nonlibrary web page
2%	Television

Prime placement on a library's web page is something everyone in the library wants for their own service. It is usually fairly easy to get the virtual reference link placed well, since it is viewed as a service that brings in new users, and helping users is a mission of most libraries. A nice logo helps draw patrons' eyes to the link.

Ubiquity of the link is another factor. The more consistently the virtual reference link is present in library web pages and even in the online catalog and databases, the more chances patrons have of seeing it when they need it. The point-of-need aspect is important. Libraries with data related to referring URLs have found that as high as one-fourth of their traffic is directed from their library catalog. A link on the home page alone is unlikely to catch the patron having difficulty finding a book or article.

Effective Strategies

Below are some strategies that many libraries have used to make their marketing efforts more effective.

Cross-Advertising: Advertise All Reference Services

Take advantage of a marketing campaign to raise the profile of all your library's reference services. Think of them as one service and promote it as having a new aspect. Or, promote the virtual reference service, but include other ways to contact the library. Advertise a single easy-to-remember URL that leads to all your reference services. Place the newest service component or the one you want to promote the most at the top of that web page.

Use your staff to promote your service. If they are enthusiastic, they will talk about your services. An in-person patron might be told about the virtual reference option or pick up a card at the desk. Virtual patrons may be told that they can call or visit the library during the same hours they can reach the library online. Low use is sometimes just low awareness. I like to promote our virtual reference service to in-library patrons, not because I think it is a better form of communication but because I know that many of our patrons are likely to next visit the library from their computers. Part of making patrons aware that we can offer help to them wherever they are is being present everywhere and cross-advertising our services.

Branding

Create a brand for your service, something identifiable and descriptive. Maryland's AskUsNow! and QandA NJ are both memorable brands that describe what they offer. Other branding may include a specific library name, such as Illinois Wesleyan University's AskAmes service. My library chose the fairly standard "Ask a Librarian" name but uses the tagline "AskUs!" and includes "AskUs" on promotional materials and as part of our URL. A little artwork can bring life to a logo. Work the brand into new ventures such as IM screen names. Avoid using the name of your software; these are tools and the tools may change (though you hope your service will endure). Logos may change to catch trends or different demographics, but consistency in naming is crucial to brand recognition.

Hitting the Target Audience

In a study of chat services that were terminated, several librarians thought that their marketing efforts had failed to meet the target and connect with their patrons. Marketing is not just about putting the word out, but aiming in the right direction. On-campus posters do not reach distance education students. Choice of giveaways must also be in tune with the target audience; Frisbees are great for college freshmen but not as good for reaching faculty. Content and tone of the message as well as the delivery method should be appropriate to the target audience. Take into consideration that most messages end up being heard or read by a wider range of people than just your intended audience. Humor can be tricky, as can trendy language; if you choose these routes, test-run the campaign with a wide range of people to make sure the humor isn't flat or the effort to be hip out of date or annoying.

Good Design Goes a Long Way

American University in Washington, DC, launched an amazing, successful, and ongoing marketing campaign a few years ago. The design style was edgy and professional. It caught the attention of students but also was suitable for viewing by parents and donors. American University hired a designer (a former student) to design its marketing materials. One example from their marketing campaign is reproduced in figure 12-2.

Even if your library does not have a large marketing budget, good design and effective marketing can happen. Partner with a marketing or design class from your local college. Their involvement could range from screening possible giveaways and strategies devised by you and your staff to taking on the development and execution of a marketing plan or designing logos and graphics for promotional materials. If this is an appealing idea, be sure to allow enough lead time to contact the appropriate faculty members to discuss the possibility of the proposed design work being part of the next semester's coursework.

The Power of Consortia

As discussed in chapter 10, some of the most comprehensive and focused marketing campaigns have come from statewide consortia. Again, this is the power of pooled resources and, often, grant money. Maryland AskUsNow! had great success developing name recognition and use. In 2006, 13 percent of

FIGURE 12-2 MARKETING IM REFERENCE SERVICE AT AMERICAN UNIVERSITY LIBRARY

Designed by Jonathon Silberman; reproduced with permission of American University Library.

those surveyed had heard of AskUsNow! and 36 percent of those people had used it. In 2003, prior to the marketing campaign, only 8 percent had heard of it, and 21 percent of those people had used it.[3] Word of mouth may account for some of this increase over time, but the intentional marketing was a factor as well.

Learning More

Librarians are seeking to increase their skills in marketing as they see the decline in user recognition of libraries as the first stop for information. Thus, marketing is a frequent topic of programs at ALA, PLA, and state and regional conferences. Often the speakers are quite energizing and informative, so take advantage of these workshops and seminars.

Consortia and large library systems may find it worthwhile to bring in a library marketing consultant to give an on-site seminar. Other libraries are often willing to share their materials or strategies, as long as there are no copyright considerations. Strategies and guidelines are also willingly shared in the library community. Consultants Linda Wallace and Peggy Barber from Library Communication Strategies developed "10 Tips for Marketing Virtual Reference Services" after working with Northern California's Q and A Café and distributed it at the ALA national conference in Atlanta as well as online.[4]

Last Words on Marketing

- ➤ Simple is good: don't complicate your message.
- ➤ It doesn't have to be expensive, but make it attractive.
- ➤ Let virtual reference market your entire library.
- ➤ Use toolkits from a statewide service or ask another library what they did—and what you might be able to copy.
- ➤ For bigger campaigns, consider employing a consultant and designer. If you are part of a larger group (county, city, university), find out who might already be available.
- ➤ Tap the creativity of your staff or community.

Marketing can be fun for you and your library. Although marketing is a serious consideration, generating visual ideas and catchy messages may provide a fresh way of thinking about the library and its services for your staff. Not all of the work needs to rest with the library staff, however. There are many resources available to help with planning and even design. This is a great opportunity for flexing your creative thinking about partnerships. You may create some buzz about the library's new virtual reference program even before the promotional materials are revealed.

NOTES

1. Patricia H. Fisher and Marseille M. Pride, *Blueprint for Your Library Marketing Plan: A Guide to Help You Survive and Thrive* (Chicago: American Library Association, 2005).
2. P. Bromberg, personal communication, July 20, 2007.
3. Maryland Public Library Survey, "Customer Survey of Maryland Residents about Libraries, Final Report," August 4, 2006, www.maplaonline.org/dlds/adobe/survey06.pdf.
4. Linda Wallace and Peggy Barber, "10 Tips for Marketing Virtual Reference Services (VRS)," www.ssdesign.com/librarypr/content/p070802a.shtml.

CHAPTER 13

Assessment and Evaluation

HOW ARE WE DOING?

Assessment has become a buzzword lately, and with good reason. Assessment allows us to see what we are doing, how we are doing, and goals for improvement.

Methods for assessment of virtual reference are quite similar to those for in-person reference. Among the most popular are traffic patterns (number of questions asked with time and date), patron attitudes (satisfaction, reasons for use), accuracy, interpersonal elements, and question analysis (subjects, number of questions per inquiry). There are a huge number of ways a library can assess a virtual reference service and many methods for gathering and assessing data. This chapter contains a variety of resources to consult for more information on specific methods.

Assessment in reference answers one (or more) of three basic questions: what are we doing, why are we doing it, and how are we doing?

> *What* assessments examine traffic patterns and types of questions (by subject, duration, etc.). These assessments can help with the administration of a service by providing information about when to staff, who to staff with, and what training is required to answer our patrons' questions.

> *Why* questions examine patron motivations for using the service and, to some extent, patron expectations of and response to the service. *Why* questions may also assess the context around the service, such as demographics and interests of the user community and gaps between patron expectations and available services (unmet needs).

> *How* questions examine the quality or our services. Accuracy of answer is a *how* question, as are assessments that examine aspects of communication between the patron and the librarian. Measures of patron satisfaction and willingness to return also tell a library how it is doing. *How* is an important question because it determines areas for improvement and establishes a base measure from which your library can set goals.

To find meaning in the answers to the *what, why,* and *how* questions, a library also needs to be able to answer the question "What do we want to be doing?" This is an easy point to forget when faced with the data collected by virtual reference software. To be meaningful, those data must be in the context of the expectations for your virtual reference service. If you know that your virtual reference service answered one thousand questions last year but you have not determined whether one thousand is an excellent number or far short of expectations, the number has no real meaning.

Assessment is, therefore, about more than gathering numbers or responses to a survey. It is about creating a context, setting goals, and taking measures (quantitatively or qualitatively) to find out where the library is in relation to its goals.

As a look at the literature of reference assessment shows, there many ways to examine a reference service. Virtual reference increases the complexity of the options because the data are more readily available for examination. Breaking the assessment process down into pieces makes assessment both more manageable and more meaningful.

Survey the Entire Landscape

To assess a virtual reference service effectively, a library should be able to place it in the context of its other reference services. To understand the assessment of reference, the library must be able to put the results in the context of its organization and user community.

If you know your virtual reference service answered one thousand IM questions last year, what does this mean?

If you know that your library answered ten thousand total reference questions, then you now know that IM is one-tenth of your reference volume. That is more interesting and has some meaning. If you also know that you have five thousand students and five hundred faculty and staff, then you know that your library answered almost two questions for every potential patron. The meaningfulness grows the more context is provided.

Now you can compare your data with that of like institutions, if you care to do so. You can examine the number of reference questions over time, perhaps also looking at the growth or decline in enrollment. If you are answering a longitudinal trend question, what relevant events may have influenced the patterns you see? Such events might be the purchase of a collection of online journals, a new catalog, or a spike in off-campus enrollment.

Depending on the data being examined and the question being answered, the relevant context varies. When reporting your assessment results, provide only the most pertinent information. Like marketing messages, assessment reports are best kept simple.

Reference as a Single Service

I advocate viewing your library's reference service as a single service with many points of contact—regardless of how and where you staff, what software you use, and whether virtual reference is administratively a separate unit. An integrated service perspective mainstreams the virtual reference component and stabilizes its place within your organization, so goals for service quality, patron satisfaction, promotion, and the like can be unified.

This integration is particularly important in assessment. Comparative data enrich assessment for the context reasons already mentioned. Set up your data collection tools to gather data sets that can be compared as parts of a cohesive whole. If, for example, you examine length of transaction for IM inquiries, establish a similar measure for the telephone rather than quantifying subjects answered in telephone calls.

Using the assessment results to set objectives and make improvements across your reference services is another advantage of the integrated approach, and one that demands comparative data.

Of course, sometimes you will want to know information specific to a mode of communication or a particular service location. Not all data points are relevant to all services. For example, most chat reference software lets you know how many people logged out of the service before receiving an initial greeting from the librarian. It is good to know if you are missing patrons by not picking up the chats promptly, but such information is not relevant to e-mail or really even to in-person or telephone service.

Know Where You Are Now

When gathering information about your reference context, determine what it is that your library is already assessing—or at least what data your library is already collecting. A lot of collected data goes unused. Use the previous assessments or analyze the collected data to form a picture of your service—where it is now and where it has been. Looking at the historic and current data can reveal what assessments are useful and what assessments are lacking and should be on the library's list for collection and evaluation.

Start with Questions

What Does Success Look Like?

Most librarians would agree that they want their service to be liked by patrons, to be used frequently, and to be accurate. Assembling a more specific picture of the successful service helps your library know how close it is to its goals. What are your goals for virtual reference volume of inquiry? At what point do you know that the service is a success? If patron satisfaction is a measure of success (which seems reasonable), how is satisfaction revealed?

Refer back to the *what, why,* and *how* questions. *What* is successful within each of these categories? Answering one thousand questions a year may be an established success measure for the second year of your service. *Why* is often established prior to the start of a service but can also be a measure of success, for instance, a goal of 20 percent of patrons using the service because they learned about it from a friend or teacher. You might determine that success means that 78 percent of the virtual reference patrons are pleased with the service they received. (These are examples only—not real success measures for any specific library.)

What Do You Want to Know?

Make sure you know what you are after. This seems obvious, once stated, but is something many people miss with assessment. They are stuck in patterns of collecting the same data, even though purposes have changed. Or they focus on what is easy to collect (see below) instead of working from what they want to know to develop an assessment plan and collect appropriate data.

Another way to state this question is "What do you want to use it for?" Several years ago I was posed this question by a colleague. I had determined that I wanted to change our primary data collection tool, but I could not figure out what changes to make. I could see myriad options for what could be collected. Over coffee, this wise friend asked what I wanted from the data—how I would put it to use. That was an easy question to answer. I wanted to know if there were hours where we were understaffed and hours where we could staff less, so that I could schedule staff where they were most needed. This was not the end of the process for assessment planning, but it was a much improved starting point.

So, what does your library want to know? Do you want to know when patrons are asking questions? What communication modes they are using? Do you want to know why they choose a form of communication, or how satisfied they are with your reference service? How do you intend to use the results of the answers to these interesting questions?

Determine Appropriate Methods of Assessment

Set Objectives and Metrics

Objectives provide a tangible structure for our goals. They provide a direction and a way to measure progress. For the goal of improving virtual reference service, an objective might be to decrease the time-to-response for e-mail questions. This is specific and well enough defined that it can be worked toward. Working toward an objective usually means having a baseline understanding of where your library currently is in relation to the objective. It is difficult to reach the finish if you can't find the starting line.

Objectives need a measurable component. An objective to provide the best reference service in the state is not measurable. How can you measure "best" and how would you collect comparative information from other services? A measurable objective might be to improve patron perceptions of the virtual reference service. This might be measured through use of a survey of patron satisfaction.

Metrics supply a concrete measure for the objective. They are usually raw numbers or percentages. Even when the data are qualitative, such as patron satisfaction, metrics can provide a goal—such as a 10 percent improvement or 70 percent of patrons responding "very satisfied" or "mostly satisfied" with the service. When setting metrics, determine two or three different benchmarks. The lowest metric indicates if you are meeting a basic level of success and the higher metrics set goals to be obtained.

Be realistic. There should be an attainable goal in every objective and metric. Do not set the first metric so high as to be discouraging. Encourage improvement and success, but don't require perfection from the start.

Measure the Right Thing

The trickiest assessment question is "Will the data we are collecting answer our question?" Particularly when a librarian is new to assessment, this one proves difficult to determine. A test collection of data is useful to determine if the assessment is on track. Early in my career, I attempted to assess the level of difficulty of questions answered at the reference desk. My instrument—librarian ranking of difficulty—was flawed. It was seeking a fairly objective measure, but librarians answered according to how difficult the question was for them. Thus, less experienced staff members were more likely to rate as difficult questions that experienced librarians rated as easy or of intermediate difficulty. This did not yield any valuable information.

Easy vs. Difficult

Some data are easy to collect. The virtual reference software may even collect it automatically and process it for you into preset reports. This is easy. What is easy, however, is not always what is good (although virtual reference vendors have worked with their customers to determine the most needed reports). Statistics are generally easy to collect, even when they are not automatic.

The data that are easy to collect often do not answer the more complex questions. For example, we may know how many questions our library answered, but not the subjects or the accuracy of our answers. This type of information requires reaching deeper into the transcripts and doing qualitative analysis. Qualitative assessment takes more time but adds dimension to what we know about our services.

Using the Results

Since a good assessment is designed to answer a question and provide useful information, the loop should be closed by using the results to make improvements to the service. Assessment may signal that it is time for a change and the direction that change should take. The library at the University of Minnesota, Mankato, examined its traffic patterns to determine both that it could change the staffing model for virtual reference and that it should increase the hours of the service; see the Library Field Report "The Slow Road to Chat."

Assessment may show patterns or trends that in turn lead to other questions. A change in the busiest time of day may indicate a needed shift in staffing patterns but may also lead the library to examine why the change occurred to be able to predict future changes. My library experienced a dramatic loss of volume on certain winter evenings, and the pattern matched collegiate basketball games—our team was highly ranked that year. We figure that if our football team were to gain such a standing, we could proactively adjust staffing levels.

Long-Range Planning

There are a variety of angles to take when evaluating a service. Trying to tackle everything at once is overwhelming and may not achieve the desired outcomes. Answering the following basic questions can help you develop a long-range assessment plan:

How much time do you have? Everyone's time is limited—even the time of dedicated assessment librarians, to which few of us have access anyway. Grand assessment plans can be made, but examine what the staff and the person leading the assessment can handle. Staff can burn out on seemingly endless data collection and become resentful or lax. Data collection should never be such a labor as to take focus away from service to the patron. Patrons can also experience assessment fatigue, particularly with surveys, and participation will decline.

The Slow Road to Chat: A Medium-Sized Academic Library's Gradual Approach to Implementing a Virtual Reference Service

Minnesota State University, Mankato, has an enrollment of about 14,000 students in 120 undergraduate and 63 graduate programs. Most courses are taught on campus, but the university has a long tradition of offering courses via interactive television and at off-campus locations, particularly in the Twin Cities, about 75 miles from Mankato. In recent years the university's distance learning offerings have grown substantially, with web-based courses replacing interactive television as the preferred delivery mode.

Our road to chat reference was a gradual one. Although the reference team was encouraged by the library administration to explore chat reference, we were not pressured to do so. We were able to discuss the merits and feasibility of chat within our existing reference context and to start the service slowly. In 2001 our former reference coordinator oversaw a short-term chat pilot project using Docutek software. The reference team then conducted a more detailed investigation of chat software providers and continued discussions about the benefits of chat reference. In 2003 the library began subscribing to QuestionPoint, and we launched our chat service in fall of that year.

Initially, we offered the QuestionPoint chat service for a few set hours each week. Some of us questioned the efficacy of this approach. We wondered if anyone would truly use a service that was offered only two or three hours a day. One of the reasons libraries were entering the chat arena was for convenience. How convenient was a service if it had such limited hours? On the other hand, many of us wondered how we could provide more extensive coverage without expanding our staff. In the end, we learned that offering chat service for a few scheduled hours a day was a workable approach. During the first two semesters of the service we offered chat for about 12 hours per week and needed only three or four librarians to staff these hours. Students discovered and used the new chat service. Our chat software provided us with good statistics and data. We knew we were picking up both repeat and new users.

In the second year of the service we expanded the service to 20 hours per week. We were able to accomplish this with the participation of additional volunteers from the reference team librarians. Participating librarians monitored the chat service from their offices during scheduled hours. The expanded service hours brought more users. However, when we examined the usage data, we discovered that we were only averaging one chat question for every three hours of scheduled service. We soon concluded that it would be feasible to monitor the chat service from the reference desk if all reference team members participated. We would also be able to offer more chat service hours each week. The librarians who had not been participating in chat trained and practiced with other team members until they were comfortable with the software.

Today we offer chat service for more than 40 hours per week during the academic year. All ten members of our reference team participate while staffing the reference desk. Our chat service has become much like a second phone at the reference desk.

We believe our chat service is a success. Although we have not won any contests for our service (many academic libraries entered the chat arena long before us; the number of chat questions we answer annually—505 in 2006—pales in comparison to other libraries; and chat still comprises less than 3 percent of our overall annual reference traffic), it is clear from our surveys and steadily growing usage that students love the service. Our slow approach to implementing and expanding chat service made it possible for reference team librarians to learn the chat software over time and to become comfortable with the chat technology through practice.

Mark McCullough, Reference Coordinator, Minnesota State University, Mankato

Michael Gorman, Assistant Professor, Reference Services, St. Cloud State University

Some data collections may be ongoing and others can be concentrated within a short period. Question volume may be recorded all the time; questionnaires may be sent and collected during a span of a few weeks. Transcript analysis to determine types of questions requires a lot of time per transcript but can be done as a snapshot from a week or two or from a sample of your transcripts. Consider what is achievable. For example, an assessment plan may include continuous collection of statistics and one other chosen assessment activity for each year of the plan.

What do you need to know now? The question of what you want to know has already been answered on a broad level. The "now" of it becomes a question of when you need to know in order to be more specific and set priorities. Are there critical questions that must be answered for a grant report or for your library board? Maybe you believe that adjustments to the staff model are needed before the start of the school year. If there are longitudinal data that your library would like to have, set this data collection up close to the beginning of the service.

The other side of this question is, What can wait? Other assessments can be prioritized and scheduled in to make them more manageable. This plan should be reviewed whenever a new assessment is undertaken to be sure that the questions being addressed are what are needed and priorities have not changed. Ongoing assessments should prepare your library to answer questions that might arise without the need to scramble to collect and analyze data.

Reflecting that assessment is an ongoing process, figure 13-1 includes a sample three-year assessment plan that answers several questions about the sample service.

Dealing with Unpleasant Results

When the assessment provides information that no one wants to hear, do not rationalize. Accept that the results were disappointing or not as expected. Do not choose a new method of assessment

FIGURE 13-1   SAMPLE OUTLINE FOR A HOLISTIC (AND AMBITIOUS) EVALUATION PLAN

What do we want to know about our services?

1. Are we providing correct answers?
2. Are patrons happy with our services?
3. Are we staffing in the most effective manner?

How often to measure:

Question 1: Snapshot. One-time measure (One day? A week? Random sampling?). Might repeat in subsequent years for comparison.

Question 2: Once every year or two.

Question 3: Continuous data collection for at least one year (may continue or repeat) to determine staffing needs over the course of an academic year.

Measurement instrument:

Question 1: Analysis of actual chat and e-mail transcripts. No comparison with in-person/telephone at this time.

Question 2: Survey to virtual reference users with questions about all modes of communication. Follow up with two focus groups with questions about all reference services. Planning study for "thank-yous" across all services with data collection next year.

Question 3: (1) Ongoing, daily collection of traffic statistics for all modes of communication. (2) One-week collection of questions asked through all modes of communication to analyze subject and expertise required. Librarians will log in-person and telephone questions and report difficulty of questions.

Reprinted from M. Kathleen Kern, "Looking at the Bigger Picture: An Integrated Approach to Evaluation of Chat Reference Services," *Reference Librarian* 46, nos. 95/96 (2006): 99–112. Article copies available from the Haworth Document Delivery Service: 1-800-HAWORTH. E-mail address: docdelivery@haworthpress.com.

or change the tool in an attempt to make the results more palatable during the next round of data collection. Even though this is tempting, it undermines the point. Make sure the collection instrument was designed to capture what you wanted, but do not assume that unsatisfactory results mean a bad assessment design. Additional assessments of analysis may be needed to determine why the objective was not met.

Unexpected or dismaying results in one area may actually indicate success in another. This is another place where understanding the broader context of your library is important. That drop in questions during the spring semester? That was when the library implemented a federated search tool. Maybe searching is easier, so questions are fewer.

What initially seems like a failure to meet a goal may in fact reveal that there are other forces at work. Maybe there is a trend or event that is off the library's radar. Question volume remained level overall, but IM questions dropped precipitously? Maybe the newest hot web browser does not work with IM. Maybe no one uses IM anymore because telepathy is the new communication tool of choice.

Sometimes dismal results indicate that an objective was not met rather than that your patrons are telepathic or that the new catalog is a dream. Then, the next assessment should focus on why there was a gap and how it can be closed during the next assessment cycle. For example, if the library feels that the return on investment is not enough, is there a way to reduce the costs (different staffing model, different software) or to increase the use of the service (improved marketing, different hours)? If patron satisfaction remains low, why is it low and why did the previous efforts at improvement result in little change?

When the Signs Say "No": Closing a Service

Undertaking assessment means that you may find that the service falls short of the library's definition of success. Sometimes a library look backs and says, "We set our goals too high" or "We really need to work on this" or "We need to change something about our service." Other times, the results are so far from the mark or so consistently short over time that a library must decide if the virtual reference service is viable. Let me reassure you that it is okay if the answer is "no."

The Ann Arbor Public Library discontinued a chat reference service after a little over a year. There was a very good core of users, but it was expensive in terms of customer response in relation to amount of library investment in the service. This was determined by looking at the number of questions they received online versus what they receive in-house during the day. James Rust, head of adult services, said, "Our population base is only 150,000 people. We just didn't generate the kind of traffic we thought we would from the Web. Maybe we launched it too early [2003], but I don't think so."[1]

It may be that the time was not right or the user community not a match for a virtual reference service. Closing your service now does not mean forever. Several libraries have terminated chat reference services but reopened using IM. The Library Field Report "Starting Over: From Consortial Chat to Instant Messaging" details the University of the Pacific Library's decision to restart virtual reference after closing its chat service. The questions that staff considered when contemplating another try are informative for new as well as second-attempt services. Others libraries have joined or left consortia and had an intervening period of closure. If your library closes its service, take stock of what you would do differently the next time and what it would take for a new service to be successful.

NOTE

1. James Rust, personal communication, March 6, 2007.

Starting Over: From Consortial Chat to Instant Messaging

The William Knox Holt Main Library, and its Health Sciences Branch, serves the University of the Pacific's main Stockton, California, campus. Pacific, an independent, comprehensive university, currently enrolls 3,500 undergraduates, 500 graduate students, and 600 first-time professional degree seekers at its Stockton location.

An overwhelming number of undergraduates reside on campus, while the majority of graduate and professional students, many of whom work full time or have family obligations, reside off campus and commute to take needed classes.

As a relatively new librarian on staff here, I was recently asked to establish a synchronous virtual reference presence at the Knox Holt Main Library. To get a sense of the library's history with this type of service, I interviewed my colleagues. I soon learned that the library had been a member of the AskNow 24/7 Reference Cooperative from July 2003 to March 2007, contributing two hours a week of staff time, with four Pacific librarians sharing these duties from their offices.

I also discovered that this live chat service, which saw only minimal usage by Pacific patrons, had often been hindered by technological difficulties and instructional constraints (including a mostly absent co-browsing feature). These difficulties often prevented those staffing it from providing the desired level of patron service, whether they were assisting members of the Pacific community or patrons at other institutions.

The decision to withdraw from 24/7 provided reference staff the opportunity to envision what a new synchronous virtual reference presence might look like, should they decide to implement one. Given the disappointing experience with the previous virtual reference arrangement, there was some understandable hesitancy toward starting a new service. To move past this, it was necessary to encourage staff to view any possible new service as an entity entirely separate and distinct from 24/7. Ultimately, to inform their decision to implement a new service, reference staff members asked these questions:

1. Should the library have a synchronous virtual reference presence through which Pacific librarians provide research assistance to our primary clientele (Pacific students, faculty and staff)?

When the answer to this question was a resounding "yes," staff members turned to another key question:

2. What technology will best enable us to provide such service, thus allowing us to leverage our underutilized intellectual capital here at the library most effectively?

After some discussion, it was decided that IM, due to its enormous popularity among our primary target population (college students 18–24 years old), would be the best tool for the job, and the AskPacific instant messaging service was born.

3. Should the service be staffed on or off the reference desk?

It was agreed that we would initially try staffing AskPacific from the reference desk in the Information Commons. Currently, one librarian staffs the reference desk while a Commons assistant (often a student) handles walk-up questions related to computing and printing from an adjoining desk. AskPacific is presently available 34 out of the 62 hours per week a reference librarian is on duty. If the service becomes popular with our patrons and usage is heavy (something we are hoping for), it may be necessary to revisit the staffing model and perhaps move the service off the desk.

AskPacific currently utilizes Meebo. This free, web-based product not only functions as an IM aggregator, providing easy, one-browser-screen access to all our IM accounts, but also enables anonymous (no screen name) IM through the MeeboMe embedded chat widget we put on the library's website. To brand ourselves on campus and make it easier for our patrons to reach us, we've claimed "AskPacific" as a screen name on all the major IM providers—AIM, Yahoo, MSN, and Google—thus allowing patrons to contact us through their preferred IM client.

As the only librarian on staff who has extensive experience with providing reference via IM, I have led and facilitated training efforts for my fellow librarians. Some of my colleagues had used IM before socially, but for others it was a brand new technology. Training consisted of a one-on-one meeting with each librarian (including a hands-on component in which they were able to log in to AskPacific and answer possible patron questions) as well as a larger group session in which we reviewed IM chat best practices as well as the basics of the Meebo interface.

Having previously worked in an academic library with an extremely robust and well-regarded IM service, I am excited for the possibilities here. We have already begun a sustained and intentional marketing effort to let the Pacific community know that there is now one more (powerful) way they can connect with their library to get the help they need, where and when they need it.

Michelle Maloney, Reference Librarian,
University of the Pacific Library

CHAPTER 14

The Road Ahead

NEXT STEPS AND EMERGING TECHNOLOGIES

I f you are reading this final chapter, you are probably in the process of implementing virtual reference. Or you've skipped ahead to try and get a scoop on the next hot reference technologies. If you've skipped to this chapter, that's okay: keep reading and then go back to the rest of the book for guidance on the implementation process. If you are implementing virtual reference with either commercial chat software or IM, it is good to keep an eye on the horizons of technology, though remembering that emerging trends are possibilities, not imperatives. Adopt at a pace appropriate to your users and your library.

If your library is implementing virtual reference and plans to have many years with this service ahead of you, you can also expect to take time to evaluate and improve. Offering virtual reference for several years almost guarantees a reassessment of and possibly a change in technologies used to support the service.

When looking at technology trends, remember that some trends end up being bigger than others. Decide whether you want to wait it out and see if a new technology becomes established or want to be one of the pioneers. There are advantages to both approaches. Trying something relatively untried can be exciting and invigorating. You may feel in a position with little to be lost and a lot to be gained from experimenting. Be ready to let go if the trend fizzles or if you are just too far ahead of the curve. Cornell University was a pioneer with videoconferencing in 1999 but dropped the service after a few semesters (see more on this below).

One of the most unexpected things that I've learned from working at a library with an established and high-volume virtual reference service is that it can be easier to be on the leading edge when you are starting fresh. Once there is an established user base, it becomes important to implement new technologies in a way that does not negatively affect existing users of virtual reference. This was at the core of my library's decision to implement IM while continuing to offer chat reference. Although IM volume has surpassed chat reference by more than five to one, we still see a core of chat reference clients, particularly among faculty and graduate students. Were we starting fresh with our virtual reference service in 2005, we may have implemented IM only. It is impossible to say if we would have missed the faculty user population had we implemented IM only. Our decision to run two parallel services—chat and IM—does exemplify a more cautious philosophy from where we were in 2001, when we started our chat service and felt that we had relatively little to lose.

Had I written this book a couple of years ago, I would have treated IM as an emerging technology for virtual reference. Although the technology itself was not new, its use in libraries was fledgling. That was 2005, this is now.

Although its popularity is still increasing, IM is no longer the emerging technology. It doesn't even get its own chapter here—it is just another one of the options. At the risk of making this book hopelessly out of date within months, this chapter provides an overview of some of the more emergent technologies libraries are using for virtual reference and other user-outreach activities.

Net Equals Network

The current buzz is about social networking and social software. This is the core of Web 2.0 and Library 2.0. The trends in Internet applications are toward quickly and easily changed content, participation in content creation, and creation of intellectual associations between pieces of information and social associations between people. These associations also take place between pieces of information and people, so that the creator of content and the commentator on content become linked as well. A lot has changed from the early days of the graphic web when websites were coded in HTML and pages were nearly as static and controlled as if they'd been printed on paper. Now blogs, wikis, and online communities allow creation of web content as easy as typing and saving a document. Updates can be sent through e-mail and even from mobile phones. Creation is social and shared, with content in perpetual draft.

For the library to be part of a user's social network is beyond "being where the users are." There is a degree of embeddedness that extends deeper than offering consultation hours at the local coffee shop (an idea discussed later in this chapter). To be part of a patron's social network requires that the patron acknowledge you as a part of his network.

The mechanism in most social software (such as Facebook and MySpace) is that a member invites another member to be his friend. By acknowledging the friend's request, the librarian (or library) is linked to that patron and, by extension, to all the patron's online friends in that particular piece of community software. (Networks such as MySpace and Facebook do not link to each other, so friends in one of these environments may not be friends in another.) The network of friends that is created is of the "A knows B and B knows C" variety: A may not know C but is linked to C through the intermediary of B. From a library outreach perspective, we hope that A comes to know about the library by being a friend of B, who has listed the library as part of her network. Ideally, A will then invite the library to be his friend.

Social Networking Websites

If all of this seems a little unfamiliar, and perhaps useless, consider some of the libraries that have started using online social networks to expand their presence in users' lives and some of their creative applications of the technology. For example, Brooklyn College was one of the first libraries in MySpace, creating its profile in December 2005. When I looked at this profile in June 2007, the library had 3,267 friends and, surprisingly, most of them were not librarians. This library uses its MySpace profile to announce events such as workshops and author readings.[1] Its friends are notified each time the library updates its profile, which draws users back to the library's MySpace presence and potentially into the (physical or virtual) library. Since MySpace is popular right now, it provides an aura of hipness that may be lacking in users' perceptions of the library. In web parlance, a profile in an online network can make the library "sticky," meaning that users return to it.

The uses of online social software go beyond marketing and outreach. There are applications that can be imbedded into a profile to allow users to do such things as search the library's online catalog, IM the library, or find articles using a federated search.

Some librarians have wondered if it is an invasion of user space—an unwelcome intrusion— for library services to be marketed to users in what is their social space. Beth Evans, a librarian at Brooklyn College says, "MySpace is an environment where people typically have other people knocking on their door and saying 'Hey, let's be friends.' Librarians may not feel comfortable doing that, but it's acceptable behavior or comfortable behavior in that environment."[2]

As to libraries wondering if it is advisable to be part of this social space, my opinion is that library presence is no more intrusive than the library building itself; patrons still have to find you the first time, and after that they still have to care to return. If they decide that they don't want the library as part of their network, it is entirely in their power to remove it as a friend. As long as you don't do anything socially unacceptable like spamming your entire network, your library will probably be just fine as a member of a social website.

Gaming Environments

Much has been written lately about how children in the United States are growing up on gaming. A fall 2003 study of the Kaiser Family Foundation showed that 44 percent of children age 0–6 had used a computer to play a game.[3] Electronic games have come a long way since Pong and Super Mario. Along with improved graphics and more sophisticated gameplay, developers have created immersive environments that include social interaction among players as a significant component. In some cases the environment and the social interaction *are* the game. It is probably more appropriate to think of websites like Second Life as online environments rather than games, although they seek to appeal to the same audience.

Libraries have entered Second Life to offer reference hours and to build collections and exhibits. The Alliance Library System (Illinois) manages Information Island, or Second Life Library 2.0, and coordinates librarians from across the country to staff reference hours. Cybrary City, which is located on Info Island, represents many libraries.[4] As new online environments are developed, libraries may choose to participate in those as well. It is interesting to note that the average age of Second Life users is 33 years.[5] It will also be interesting to see how use of these environments expands and if they become more mainstream ways to visit business and cultural institutions.

Hear Me, See Me, Text Me

Text Messaging

Text messaging is hugely popular in parts of the world. In particular, it has taken hold in Europe and East Asian countries. In the United States, about 60 percent of young adults 18–29 send or receive text messages daily, compared to 32 percent of those age 32–49 (Generation X).[6] Text messaging in the United States nearly doubled from 2005 to 2006, from 81 billion to nearly 158.6 billion messages.[7] This is another technology that is particularly prevalent among younger populations in the United States and is predicted to expand in use as today's teenagers become older and new young people grow up using text messaging.

The implications for libraries are still unclear. Libraries have begun to design mobile web pages, aimed at people who web-browse from their handhelds and mobile phones. In terms of virtual reference, messages sent via the SMS (Short Message Service) technology are usually limited to 160 characters, which is quite small for communicating library information or even for asking questions. Multiple messages can be sent, but a string of instructions sent this way is likely to be an annoyance for the librarian and the patron. Factual information such as a call number or hours for the library can be easily communicated within one text message. As mentioned earlier in this book, virtual reference services have found that patrons ask the same types of questions through virtual reference they ask in person, but it is unclear if this would hold true for SMS. With the strictness of the limitations on message size, it is possible that users may be more selective about what they ask. Libraries would also need to be selective about how they answer and somehow make clear what they are willing to answer. Asking for the title of an article supporting gun control may seem acceptable to a student and can be asked and answered in 160 characters, but most academic libraries would not send a response that chose specific articles for the student. At the same time, 160 characters do not allow room for the library to provide instruction on how the patron can search for articles himself. This could cause discontent or confusion on the part of the patron.

The library at Southeastern Louisiana University (SELU) added text messaging to its suite of virtual reference services in 2005. Their SMS service converts the patron's text message, which is then sent to a library text-only telephone number and then to an e-mail that is received by the library. The library responds with an e-mail (keeping it within the 160-character limit), and the e-mail is converted to a text message that is sent to the user. The SELU library found that patrons asked all types of questions, from facts about the library and campus to simple library questions and even complex research questions. Still, an overwhelming majority of questions (91 percent) were from "patrons who were asking questions where they realistically could expect a brief answer. Students who text message seem to understand the limits of the technology and tend to ask questions that they believe will be answered with a short reply."[8] In a presentation about the pilot phase of this service, J. B. Hill, head of reference at SELU, noted that a cause of low use may be that users find IM and e-mail to be more convenient text-based ways to reach the library. It was easy for the library to incorporate text messaging into its workflow, however, so low use of the service was not seen as a reason to discontinue it.[9]

The Orange County (Florida) Library System has made good use of SMS technology by setting up quick "keyword services" that allow the user to send a very short query to find library branches by ZIP code or find the address by entering the branch library's name. It also has a good FAQ about the SMS service (www.ocls.info/xplor/faqs.asp). In short, SMS seems a technology about which libraries should keep current, and a few adventurous ones will pioneer it as a service and work out the rough spots so that the road is easier to travel if it becomes a mainstream library service.

VoIP and Other Audio

The important points in recent developments related to online voice communications are inter-operability with the telephone, integration with text-based systems such as IM and call center software, and improved synchronization between audio and video components in videoconferencing. As discussed in chapter 6, VoIP has widespread use in the general population and growing use by corporate call centers.

Videoconferencing

Taking the idea of enriching online communications by providing an experience more like that of face-to-face communications a step further, some libraries have forayed into reference through videoconferencing. The libraries at Cornell University were perhaps the earliest to adopt video to enhance online communications. They initiated a pilot in 1997, using the CUSeeMe software to provide service from one library (Olin) where there were librarians to another (Uris) that was not staffed with librarians during the evening. Students could approach a dedicated terminal in Uris that had the CUSeeMe software installed and communicate with a librarian at a desk in Olin. The intent was to "replicate as completely as possible the in-person interaction, especially the reference interview," according to Nancy Skipper, a librarian at Cornell University's Olin Library.[10]

This pilot lasted two semesters, and then other means of providing online reference were pursued. Much about the demise of this pilot is linked to it being a very new technology and one unfamiliar to both librarians and, more important, patrons. Still, it provided some lessons for libraries considering using video technologies that are now a decade more advanced. During an interview, Skipper shared that

> ultimately, our decision to bring the project to an end was based on the difficulty of responding to questions in person while being suddenly contacted through video conferencing. There was no way to queue the interactions. We also got some very odd looks from patrons nearby who observed us, apparently, talking to our computer at the reference desk.

Skipper noted, however, that some of these challenges were similar to ones that occur with chat reference staffing models today when libraries try to manage chat at a service desk. These are certainly considerations that hold true today for any library preparing to meet patrons face to face in cyberspace: it is one thing to IM while at the desk and another to appear to talk to yourself at the desk, and it may not be as easy to queue two essentially face-to-face patrons.

A few other libraries since Cornell have tried videoconferencing with patrons, but this technology has not found a foothold in library reference. Perhaps it is, as Skipper noted, that "people are so comfortable now with typing back and forth through instant messaging and chat."

The appeal of adding video and audio enhancements is the more context-rich and immersive experience for both patron and librarian. Whereas librarians see a clear use for the verbal and visual cues provided by voice and video, it is not yet clear if these are features patrons would find equally useful.

Getting Away from the Desk

Okay, this is not really a technology, but it is worth mentioning in any contemporary book on reference service. The point of virtual reference is to be where the users are. Look at where else (besides online and in your library) your users are congregating to do their homework and conduct their research. Are there other places where the library can offer reference, and can these fit the librarians' schedules? Maybe a lobby coffee shop in an academic building, or within your own library building? Or a few hours a week at a dormitory computer lab? If there is a bank of computers in your library that is busy, consider roaming to see if anyone needs assistance. Librarians sometimes fear this approach as too sales-like, aggressive, or a set-up for rejection. Anecdotally, about one of every three people I ask "Are you finding what you need?" requests assistance with a search or has some other library question but has not approached the reference desk. And only once has someone been offended that I asked. I do take care to not approach those who clearly do not need assistance—those users checking e-mail or playing games. I concentrate on those who I can see are using the library's catalog or online databases. The University of Alberta is merging the concepts of virtual reference and in-person reference with their Cameron Help service. Patrons present in the library are encouraged to use IM to page a librarian to come to where they are (in a five-floor building) and confer with them in person.

On Moving Forward

I hope that your librarians find virtual reference to be a rewarding experience and that your patrons find it useful. It may even be a fun experience for everyone. As one New Jersey patron opined, "I am ecstatic about the whole darn thing."[11] It is difficult to be indifferent in the face of such enthusiasm.

NOTES

1. MySpace describes profiles to its new users as "Your Space on the Web, where you can describe yourself, hobbies and interests. You can even upload pics and write journals." A profile is an individual page within a social networking site that is created and maintained by a user of the site. It is most often publicly available on the social network and essentially represents the user as an individual in that virtual space. A profile exists so that a user can make himself or herself known to other users. It most often includes personal information about the user's geographic location, education, occupation, hobbies, and interests. Profiles may be used to post blog or journal entries, photos or videos, or announcements to public bulletin boards. A profile also commonly contains a section that publicly displays thumbnail images of each of the "friends" the profiled user has within the network, each of which provides a link to those individuals' profiles.

2. Beth Evans, e-mail to M. K. Kern, March 27, 2007.

3. Victoria J. Rideout, Elizabeth A. Vandewater, and Ellen A. Wartella, "Zero to Six: Electronic Media in the Lives of Infants, Toddlers and Preschoolers," Report from the Henry J. Kaiser Family Foundation, October 28, 2003, www .kff.org/entmedia/upload/Zero-to-Six-Electronic-Media-in-the-Lives-of-Infants-Toddlers-and-Preschoolers-PDF.pdf (p. 14).

4. More about Information Island and Cybrary City can be found at http://infoisland.org/about/ and www.libsuc cess.org/index.php?title=Cybrary_City.

5. Adam Reuters, "Europe Takes Lead in Second Life Users," *Reuters: Second Life News Center,* February 9, 2007, http://secondlife.reuters.com/stories/2007/02/09/europe-takes-lead-in-second-life-users/.

6. John Horrigan, "Mobile Access to Data and Information," Report from Pew Internet and American Life Project, March 2008, www.pewinternet.org/pdfs/PIP_Mobile.Data.Access.pdf.

7. Tracey Wong Briggs, "15 Years after Birth, Book's Not Closed on Texting," *USA Today,* September 3, 2007, www .usatoday.com/tech/news/2007-09-03-texting-language_N.htm.

8. J. B. Hill, Cherie Madarash Hill, and Dayne Sherman, "Text Messaging in an Academic Library: Integrating SMS into Digital Reference," *Reference Librarian* 47, no. 97 (2007): 17–29.

9. J. B. Hill. "Text a Librarian: Integrating Reference by SMS into Digital Reference," presented at the Virtual Reference Desk Conference 2005, http://data.webjunction.org/wj/documents/12542.pdf.

10. Nancy Skipper, interview with Lena Singer, June 22, 2007. For a more recent example of a videochat service, see Char Booth, "Developing Skype-Based Reference Services," *Internet Reference Services Quarterly* 13, no. 2–3 (2008): 147–165.

11. Karen Hyman and Peter Bromberg, "I'm Just Ecstatic about the Whole Darn Thing! Customer Feedback and Lessons Learned at QandA NJ, New Jersey's 24/7 Live Virtual Reference Service," Virtual Reference Desk Conference, 2003, available at www.qandanj.org/vrd/.

appendix A

Guidelines for Implementing and Maintaining Virtual Reference Services

Prepared by the MARS Digital Reference Guidelines Ad Hoc Committee, Reference and User Services Association, 2004. Approved by the RUSA Board of Directors in June 2004. Published in *Reference and User Services Quarterly* 44, no. 1 (2004): 9–14.

Introduction

Technological developments have affected not only the format and sources of the information libraries use to provide reference service, but also where we provide reference service. Libraries and their resources have partially moved to the virtual world of the Internet. As a result, library patrons can access our resources from outside of the physical library. In an effort to reach patrons accessing the library via their computers, many libraries and library consortia are extending their reference service to include virtual reference. Technology now allows users to submit their queries to the library at any time from any place in the world. Virtual reference is responsive to patrons' need for convenient access to reference service.

The purpose of these guidelines is to assist libraries and consortia with implementing and maintaining virtual reference services. The guidelines are meant to provide direction, without being overprescriptive. Variance among institutions will result in differences in the adherence to these guidelines, but the committee hopes to have cast the model broadly enough to provide a framework for virtual reference which can be widely adopted and which will endure through many changes in the ways in which libraries provide virtual reference services.

The committee first based these guidelines on the Bernie Sloan article, "Electronic reference services: Some suggested guidelines" which appeared in *Reference and User Services Quarterly*, Volume 38, Number 1, Summer 1998, p. 77–81.

RUSA hopes the following guidelines will be useful to anyone attempting to formalize a virtual reference service.

1 Definition of Virtual Reference

1.1 Virtual reference is reference service initiated electronically, often in real-time, where patrons employ computers or other Internet technology to communicate with reference staff, without being physically present. Communication channels used frequently in virtual reference include chat, videoconferencing, Voice over IP, co-browsing, e-mail, and instant messaging.

1.2 While online sources are often utilized in provision of virtual reference, use of electronic sources in seeking answers is not of itself virtual reference.

1.3 Virtual reference queries are sometimes followed-up with telephone, fax, in-person and regular mail interactions, even though these modes of communication are not considered virtual.

2 Preparing for Virtual Reference Services

2.1 Virtual reference should be undertaken with a view to the long-term integration of the service with the rest of the institution's reference services. Even at the planning or pilot phases, virtual reference should not be treated as an ad hoc service.

2.2 Administration should be aware of the staffing, start-up and maintenance costs involved in providing and marketing virtual reference and should be prepared to commit to long-term provision of resources.

2.3 Ideally, all levels of the institution's management should commit to supporting virtual reference before the service is formalized. As with any new service, total support from all members of management may not be possible; however, there should be a sufficient core of staff committed to providing a virtual reference service.

2.4 Representative members of the administration and reference library staff should be involved in planning, training, implementation, and promotion of virtual reference services and the selection of virtual reference software. Representative members of the target audience should be involved in planning and promotion of virtual reference.

2.5 Relevant computing staff should be involved in the planning, implementation, and maintenance of the infrastructure needed, and in the software selection and purchase decision, particularly with regard to compatibility with existing library software and infrastructure.

2.6 Virtual reference service should be a consideration in collection development decisions, selection of electronic reference sources, and especially licensing issues that might affect use of resources to serve off-site patrons.

2.7 Library staff and administration should facilitate regular assessment of the program's effectiveness and commit to adjustments as needed. Assessment should be comparable to the assessment of other reference services.

3 Provision of Service

3.1 Clientele

    3.1.1   The library should define the patron population and publicize this policy on the service's Web site, or other places where patrons may access it.

    3.1.2   Technical issues of patron authentication or proxy server login should be addressed as they apply to various groups within the patron population.

    3.1.3   If there are persons excluded from this service by institutional policy, enforcement should be uniform.

    3.1.4   Guidelines for appropriate behavior while using the service should be made available to patrons.

    3.1.5   Marketing of the service should clearly define the target audience.

3.2 Parameters of Service

    3.2.1   The level of service to be provided should be defined and announced, so that staff and patrons will understand the mission of the service. Level of service includes the types of questions the service will answer (perhaps easier to define in the negative), as well as the patron population the service will serve.

    3.2.2   Guidelines should be established for determining which queries fall outside the parameters of service, and how to respond in those cases.

    3.2.3   Before the service begins, it should be decided if document delivery will be included and whether patrons will be charged for document delivery.

    3.2.4   Parameters of time should be determined and announced to both patrons and staff. For synchronous virtual reference, the times at which the service is staffed should be indicated. For asynchronous virtual reference, guidelines for how frequently queries will be checked, or how soon an initial response can be expected, should be given.

    3.2.5   Internal and external links to the virtual reference service should be designed to catch the attention of potential patrons and to clearly communicate the nature of the service.

3.3 Service Behaviors

    3.3.1   Virtual reference requires of library staff many of the same communication and interpersonal skills necessary for other forms of reference. The absence of a physically present patron and the different modes of communication may call for additional skills, effort, or training to provide quality service on par with face-to-face reference services.

    3.3.2   Staff should exhibit the professional competencies essential for successful reference and patron services librarians, as articulated in RUSA's "Professional Competencies for Reference and User Services Librarians."

3.3.3 Standard guidelines of reference service (such as reference interviewing, exchange of questions between services, et al.) should prevail.

3.3.4 Staff should follow interpersonal communication practices that promote effective provision of reference service, as articulated in the RUSA "Guidelines for Behavioral Performance of Reference and Information Services Professionals."

3.3.5 Staff should be required to demonstrate skills in the effective use of online communication, as well as demonstrate awareness of the common potential problem areas when conducting reference interviews online, as compared to the face-to-face reference interview.

3.3.6 Initial and ongoing training should be offered to help staff learn and retain these effective online behaviors.

3.3.7 Staff should treat patrons' and colleagues' online communication, including stored transcripts or records, as private and confidential.

3.4 Collaborative Virtual Reference

3.4.1 Some libraries may choose to provide virtual reference services collaboratively with other libraries, for various reasons including: to extend their hours of operation, to distribute staffing of the service across multiple libraries, to extend the expertise available, or to realize cost saving associated with economies of scale. Such collaboration may include working with virtual reference vendors, and/or participation in large regional or national collaborations.

3.4.2 Expectations for libraries participating in a collaborative service should be clearly defined before the local library commits to such a service.

3.4.3 Responsibility for centrally administering and coordinating the service should be clearly defined.

3.4.4 Each library should have a project liaison to represent the library in the group's activities. Expectations for project liaison's duties should be clearly stated.

3.4.5 Procedures for communications between and among participants should be clearly delineated.

3.4.6 Participating libraries should commit to a prescribed minimum level of service. For synchronous virtual reference, this level of service should be a set minimum number of service hours, based upon factors such as size of library or staff, patron population being served, budget, and extent of online reference service desired. For asynchronous virtual reference, this level of service should be a prescribed minimum number of questions to be handled or monitoring of the queue for specific blocks of time.

3.4.7 Scheduling of libraries' contributions to the service should be centrally administered. For synchronous virtual reference, each library should commit to specific blocks of time. Finding specific reference staff to fill these blocks of time should be the responsibility of the local library, and not that of the project director. For asynchronous virtual reference, participating libraries should commit to monitoring question queues for incoming questions in specific blocks of time.

3.4.8   The service should provide a central source of information on member library policies, operations, procedures, and regulations, so that it is simple for project reference staff to find information about other libraries.

3.4.9   The service should establish a clear set of guidelines for establishing priorities for service for patrons from the various libraries, e.g., in a collaborative virtual reference service; questions are handled on a first-come-first-served basis, with no preference given to patrons from the on-duty staff's own local library.

3.4.10   The service should establish clear policies and guidelines for using licensed online electronic resources to serve patrons from other participating libraries.

3.4.11   The service should establish clear policies and guidelines that effectively ensure patron privacy in a multi-library setting.

3.4.12   Observance of the NISO Question/Answer Transaction Protocol for transferring questions between services is encouraged.

4 Organization of Service

4.1 Integration of Virtual Reference Service

4.1.1   Virtual Reference is an extension of an institution's existing reference services. While staffing models and the location of the service may be different from face-to-face reference services, it should be accorded the same status and quality goals and be viewed as a part of the larger service of reference.

4.1.2   All public services staff should have an awareness of the virtual reference service's goals and basic operation.

4.1.3   Procedures should be established for referring a virtual patron (question) to another reference or public services point. Procedures should include both how the referral is presented to the patron and how information about the referral is communicated between the virtual reference desk and referral destination.

4.2 Infrastructure/Facilities

4.2.1   It is a goal of all reference services to be of high quality. Integration of virtual reference into the mainstream of reference services implies that all services (in-person, telephone, and virtual) will be supported at a level to ensure quality service.

4.2.2   Each library should examine staffing models to determine one that is appropriate for their organization. While there is not a "one-size-fits-all" service model, a model should be chosen which would support quality reference interactions via all modes of communication.

4.2.3   Staff should be provided space, furnishings, hardware, and software to accomplish the mission agreed on by staff, administration, and technological support staff.

4.2.4 Equipment, facilities, and software should be updated as needed to maintain efficacy. Planning should take into account the continuing evolution of technology.

4.2.5 Awareness of the patrons' infrastructure and capabilities should be taken into account when planning library capabilities and choosing virtual reference software.

4.2.6 Technical set-up should take into consideration use of the supporting software by patrons and reference staff with disabilities. Some options include choosing software that complies with section 508 of the Rehabilitation Act, software with non-text options such as voice-over-IP, or providing text on the Web site that directs screen-readers to an e-mail form or alternate contact information.[1]

4.3 Finances

4.3.1 The library budget should include specific allocation of funds to cover the personnel, hardware, software, connectivity, furnishings, training, publicity, and space to support this service.

4.3.2 Planning should include ongoing budgeting even when the service is started as a pilot or with seed money from a grant.

4.3.3 Whether the service is to be free to the patron or fee-based should be determined before the service begins and modified as needed.

4.4 Personnel

4.4.1 Virtual reference service responsibilities should be shared among staff to ensure continuity of service.

4.4.2 When possible, staff should be trained for all reference services (face-to-face and virtual) to provide greater depth of knowledge and flexibility for staffing.

4.4.3 Library staff conducting virtual reference should be selected on the basis of ability, interest, and availability. Service behaviors as described in section 3.3 and skills to use the supporting technology need to be part of staff selection.

4.4.4 Staff should be provided time and resources for training and continuing education to ensure effective service.

4.5 Marketing

4.5.1 A marketing plan should be developed and implemented as part of the planning and ongoing operation of the service.

4.5.2 A target audience or audiences for the virtual reference service should be determined and marketing should be appropriate to that audience. Members of the target audience should be included in the planning and evaluation of marketing.

4.5.3 There should be a budget for marketing and marketing should be assigned as a responsibility to a staff member or members.

4.5.4 Marketing should be routinely evaluated and updated to keep the message fresh and reach new audiences.

4.6 Evaluation and Improvement

    4.6.1   A virtual reference service should be analyzed regularly, using input from staff and patrons, to evaluate its effectiveness and efficiency, with the goal of providing a high-quality service.

    4.6.2   Evaluation may encompass many methods such as the analysis of usage statistics, patron feedback, and reviewing transcripts.

    4.6.3   Evaluation of the virtual reference service should be equivalent to and part of a library's regular evaluation of all its reference services.

    4.6.4   Evaluation should be used to improve the service as needed through adjustment of staffing, levels of staffing, service parameters, training, or other improvements as indicated by evaluation and assessment results.

5 Privacy

5.1 Virtual reference communications between patrons and library staff should be private except as required by law.

5.2 Data gathered and maintained for the purpose of evaluation should protect patrons' confidentiality.

    5.2.1   It is recommended that patrons' personal identifiers, such as name, e-mail, etc. be stripped from transaction records. Stripped records may be maintained for statistical and evaluative purposes.

    5.2.2   Libraries need to develop retention schedules and privacy policies for their virtual reference transactions.

    5.2.3   Patrons should be advised whether a record of the transaction will be retained, and what, if any, personal information will be stored with the transaction log.

    5.2.4   Privacy policies and transcript retention schedules should be publicly available.

5.3 Reference transactions may be used in the creation of databases and FAQs but care should be taken to maintain the privacy of patrons and the confidentiality of patrons' inquiries.

    5.3.1   Beyond removal of patron identifiers, inclusion in a database should not compromise patron confidentiality, and this should be evaluated when choosing questions for inclusion in a database.

    5.3.2   Patrons should be informed, through publicly available policy, that their questions might be included in a database. They should be provided a means to request removal of their inquiries from the database.

5.4 Data gathered and maintained for training purposes and for publicizing the service should also protect patron confidentiality.

MARS DIGITAL REFERENCE GUIDELINES AD HOC COMMITTEE

John Glace

M. Kathleen Kern, co-chair

Lori Morse

Janice Rice

Jana Ronan

Bernie Sloan, co-chair

Kris Stacey-Bates

NOTE

1. "Nondiscrimination under Federal grants and programs: Electronic and information technology," Title 29 U.S. Code, Pt. 794d 2004 ed.

BIBLIOGRAPHY

The NISO Question/Answer Transaction Protocol is under development at this time. Information about this protocol is available at the NISO Committee AZ Web sites.

Reference and User Services Association. *Guidelines for Behavioral Performance of Reference and Information Services Professionals.* Approved by the RUSA Board of Directors, June 2004.

Reference and User Services Association. *Professional Competencies for Reference and User Services Librarians.* Approved by the RUSA Board of Directors, January 26, 2003.

Sloan, Bernie. Electronic reference services: Some suggested guidelines. *Reference and Users Services Quarterly* 38 (1), 77-81. Summer 1998. Electronic version, reproduced with the permission of the American Library Association.

appendix B

Market Assessment

ILLUMINE LIBRARY, ERUDITION COLLEGE

APRIL 9, 2007

Description of Library

Erudition College is a four-year liberal arts college with an undergraduate population of 3,200. In addition it offers three master's programs, in education, ethnomusicology, and oil engineering. There are 160 faculty and 240 full-time staff. Library services to alumni are strong, with lifetime library cards for materials borrowing and two major online database packages available for their use. Residents of Brighton are eligible for library cards, but few take advantage of this, possibly because of the outstanding Brighton Public Library.

Illumine Library is located on the edge of campus and has a heavily used fifty-seat computer lab. The campus estimates that 70 percent of the students own laptop computers, and most of the campus (including the library) is wireless. The library is frequently busy, but there has been a steady decline in reference inquiries.

Brighton is an exurban town of 23,000. About half of the faculty live in Municity, 45 minutes away, and commute to campus several days a week. The undergraduate population is mostly residential, with 85 percent living in campus-owned housing. Each semester 450 students study abroad.

Most of the students in the master's programs, by contrast, live in Municity or one of the several rural towns within a 50-mile radius.

Population Characteristics

Age group	Number	Approx. % IM users (Pew report 200_)	Approx. % e-mail users (Pew report 200_)	Characteristics
Total population	4,200+ alumni			Lifelong library card for students/alumni.
Undergraduates (17–23)	3,200			85% on-campus housing. 450 study abroad. Traditional student body. Research-intensive coursework.
Faculty	160			50% live outside Brighton
Staff	240			Wide range of age groups and educational backgrounds.
Alumni	>40,000			Approx. 3,000–4,000 active library users.
Oil Engineering	50			Mostly age 22–30. Two years of on-campus coursework, one year and two summers of fieldwork (~200 miles from Brighton).
Ethnomusicology	35			Mainly 22–26, with a few older professional musicians. One year on-campus coursework and one year of fieldwork worldwide.
Education	120			Even mix of 22–26-year-olds and nontraditional students. Two-year program with one semester of student teaching (outside Brighton). Classes held on the Brighton campus and at a location in Municity.
Brighton residents	400			Includes family members of faculty and staff.

5-year Trends in Circulation

FY 2002	FY 2003	FY 2004	FY 2005	FY 2006	~10% decline
90,000	87,000	83,000	84,500	82,500	General downward trend started in 1996. 2004–2006 plateau trend. Increased use from alumni. Interlibrary lending figures (not included) increasing. Interlibrary borrowing steady.

5-year Trends in Reference Inquiries (by type of communication, if known)

FY 2002	FY 2003	FY 2004	FY 2005	FY 2006	~5% decline (figures exclude directional questions)
4,000	3,600	3,800	4,100	3,850	General downward trend started in 1996. 2004–2006 plateau trend. No separate statistics for modes of communication, but librarians report decrease in telephone calls and increase in e-mail. In-person a consistent 65% of inquiries.

Other Usage Data (gate counts, computer usage, database usage)

Gate counts follow general trend above. Increased with new computer lab and wireless access in FY 2005. Database usage increased dramatically (50%) since 2003, although accuracy of vendor-supplied statistics uncertain.

Current Programs for Specific Populations and Attendance

➤ Optional 2-credit library course taken by 5% of undergraduates.

➤ Strong curriculum-integrated information literacy in social science degree programs.

➤ Heavily used library gateway for off-campus students (study abroad, internships, etc.).

➤ Writing workshop located in the library assists 500 students a semester with term papers (staffed by Student Academic Affairs office).

➤ New faculty orientation has 100% attendance, and library presents an hour on library services and resources.

Other Considerations

➤ New program starting in spring 2008—free online humanities courses for alumni (may take one course a year, four courses offered each semester). Alumni enrolled able to use all databases.

➤ New college president pushing for innovation in the library and campus IT services.

Assessment

The *Undergraduate* population represents a significant target group for a new IM service because of the prevalence of IM use within this age cohort. Students using laptops are known to be reluctant to leave their seats to ask a question (or locate a book) since students vie for preferred seating in popular areas of the library. Conversely, foot-traffic analysis has revealed that students who use the reference desk in person stop on their way into the library. Few telephone and e-mail inquiries are received from on-campus undergraduates, perhaps because of the very residential nature of the student body.

Off-campus Study Abroad students are known to be heavy users of the library from their remote locations, as demonstrated by the website visits to the off-campus library portal and the numbers of e-mails from this group.

The *Education* and *Oil Engineering* programs present target communities because of their distance and advanced research needs. It is known that the oil engineers have laptops in the field and that the education program requires many research projects as well as curriculum planning activities. *Ethnomusicology* fieldwork is mostly in countries with limited Internet access, and the study is largely immersion and observation of the culture.

The commuter nature of the *Faculty* may make this a target population. Currently this group e-mails the library with regularity. There is some doubt about adoption of IM within this community. *Staff* who conduct research for faculty and those in administration are known users of telephone reference. It is perceived as unlikely that they will opt to contact the library via IM because of the median age of this group.

Alumni who are current users of the library, as well as those who might take the free online courses, are logical users of this service. E-mail may be preferred over IM, however, depending on age. It is expected that library use by this group will increase over the next few years and that questions about library technology will predominate.

Community Users are not a significant percentage of Illumine Library users and are not expected to make extensive use of an IM service. Although IM could be an outreach opportunity to this group, it may be impolitic to seem in competition with the public library.

Conclusions

There is sufficient potential audience for IM for the Erudition College librarians to pilot an IM service. The target groups (at least initially) will be the education and oil engineering master's students, the off-campus undergraduates, and the alumni enrolled in the free online courses. Marketing to faculty and on-campus undergraduates will be less intense than to these groups, although all users will be welcome to use the IM service. Links to the virtual reference services (IM and e-mail) will be placed on all library web pages, and the service will be mentioned in new faculty orientation and library instructional sessions.

appendix C

Preparing for Virtual Reference: A Checklist

Use this checklist to keep track of your implementation process and as a guide to the other documentation you create. For reference, appropriate chapters, worksheets, exercises, and VR Guidelines sections are noted in brackets.

PREPARING FOR VIRTUAL REFERENCE

Decision to consider implementation [chapter 2, esp. worksheet 2-1]

_____

_____

Market Assessment [chapter 3, esp. worksheet 3-1; Guidelines 3.1]

_____

_____

Determination of appropriate audience(s)

_____

_____

Met with stakeholders (who, role, date) [chapter 4; Guidelines section 2]

_____

_____ etc.

Commitment obtained from / nature of commitment:

_____

_____ etc.

Agreement on service philosophy [chapter 5, esp. exercise 5-1]

_____

_____

Policies and parameters of service written [chapter 5, esp. exercise 5-2; Guidelines 3.1–3.2 and section 5]

_____

_____

Evaluated software xyz [chapter 6, esp. worksheet 6-1]

Software name: _____ Feedback obtained from: _____

Software name: _____ Feedback obtained from: _____

Software name: _____ Feedback obtained from: _____

Software chosen: _____

Staffing model chosen [chapter 8; Guidelines 4.1–4.2, 4.5] _____

_____

Budget determined [chapter 9, esp. worksheet 9-1; Guidelines 4.3, also 4.1–4.2 and section 2]

Sources of funding _____

Collaboration decision made [chapter 10; Guidelines 3.4]

    Possible collaborations considered_____

_____

    Collaboration: Yes or No?

    If yes, name of collaboration and contact person _____

_____

    Training (who, what, when) [chapters 7 and 11; Guidelines 3.3] _____

_____

_____

_____

Marketing plan written [chapter 12; Guidelines 4.5]

    Methods: _____

    Time line: _____

    People responsible: _____

Assessment plan written (3 year) [chapter 13; Guidelines 4.6]

    Year 1 methods _____

    Who is involved_____

    Time line(s) _____

    Follow-up on results_____

    Follow-up implemented _____

    Year 2 methods_____

_____ etc.

index

Note: Page numbers in italics indicate the VR Guidelines in appendix A.

online communication skills
  and consortia, 93
  making up for lack of vision or voice, 65–69
  styles of, 63–65
  training in, 100
  in VR guidelines, *129, 130*
open-source applications, 59–60
Orange County (Fla.) Library System, 124
organization of service, *131–132. See also* staffing models
output data and costs, 84
outreach, 125

P

page pushing, 52
paging services, 125
parameters of service, *129*
patron attitudes in assessment, 109
patron behavior, 69, 70, 71, *129*
patrons
  comfort with older technologies, 120
  communication with, 61–71; exercise, 62
  conflicts with staff needs, 9, 12
  difference between chat and IM for, 50
  and need to download software, 55
  and privacy policy, 40–42
  questions for in surveys, 18
patrons without questions, communications with, 52, 69
patterns of use and hours of service, 80
peer pressure, 7
Penn State University, 36
philosophy of service, 32–33
  exercise, 34
planning, 5–14
  checklist, 139–141
  cost of, 86
  need for, 12–13
  in VR guidelines, *128*
planning, long-range, 113, 115
policies, 32–45
  in consortia, 95
  on database use in VR guidelines, *131*
  example, 39
  exercises, 34, 45
  on priority of service, 35–36, 74
  publication of, 37–38
  on response to harassing users, 44
  on scope of questions, 36, 38–40, 44
  and software selection, 55
  on time limitations, 37
  training in, 100
  on unaffiliated patrons, 33, 35, 44
  for use of free VoIP, 53
pop-up blockers, 53
pop-up windows, 24
preparation for VR, *128. See also* planning
Princeton University, 54
print resources, access to, 74
priorities
  among types of patrons, 35–36

  between in-person and virtual patrons, 35–36, 74
  of library, 8–9; worksheet, 10–11
  See also queuing
privacy
  and patron verification, 35
  policies on, 40–43
  and software capabilities, 25
  in survey design, 17
  in VR guidelines, *130, 131, 133*
promotion of library, 7. *See also* marketing
punctuation in online chat, 64
Purdue University, 80

Q

Q and A Café, 108
QandA NJ, 88, 105–106
qualitative analysis, 112–113
quality assurance and training, 101
question analysis in assessment, 109
QuestionPoint, 6, 58, 59, 88
queuing
  in collaboration, 95, *131*
  and videoconferencing, 124
  See also priorities

R

reach-out software, 52
readiness of organization to begin VR, 8–12
recurring costs, 86–87
reference interview, 63–64, 68, 71
reference services
  roaming by librarians, 125
  role of VR in, 110–112
  in VR guidelines, *130, 131*
referrals
  of difficult questions and quality control, 91
  in VR guidelines, *131*
regional libraries and incentive to begin VR, 7
reports from software, 57–58
Research Help Now, 93
results, unexpected, 115–117
results, uses of, 113
retention policy for transcripts, 41–42
roaming by librarians, 125
rude and impatient patrons, 44, 69, 70, 71

S

Samford University, 50
scheduling of services, 79
scope of questions
  and abusive patrons, 44
  out-of-scope questions, 38, 40
  policy for, 36, 38–40, 44
scripts for text message questions, 49
Second Life, 122
security
  and e-mail software, 49
  and VoIP, 53
  See also authentication of ID and privacy; privacy